Pete Buckley currently runs the mountain walking website easywayup.com and has travelled extensively in Europe as well as several forays further afield. 31 Days in a Campervan is his first book and is a personal account of the New Zealand experience seen through the eyes of a couple who love the outdoors. He is now married to Jacqui and lives in Lancashire.

31 Days in a Campervan

(Trolling around New Zealand)

By
Pete Buckley

Order this book online at www.trafford.com/07-0585
or email orders@trafford.com

Most Trafford titles are also available at major online book retailers.

© Copyright 2007 Pete Buckley.

All rights reserved. No part of this publication may be reproduced, stored in a retrieval system, or transmitted, in any form or by any means, electronic, mechanical, photocopying, recording, or otherwise, without the written prior permission of the author.

Note for Librarians: A cataloguing record for this book is available from Library and Archives Canada at www.collectionscanada.ca/amicus/index-e.html

ISBN: 978-1-4251-2183-9

We at Trafford believe that it is the responsibility of us all, as both individuals and corporations, to make choices that are environmentally and socially sound. You, in turn, are supporting this responsible conduct each time you purchase a Trafford book, or make use of our publishing services. To find out how you are helping, please visit www.trafford.com/responsiblepublishing.html

Our mission is to efficiently provide the world's finest, most comprehensive book publishing service, enabling every author to experience success. To find out how to publish your book, your way, and have it available worldwide, visit us online at www.trafford.com/10510

Trafford PUBLISHING

www.trafford.com

North America & international
toll-free: 1 888 232 4444 (USA & Canada)
phone: 250 383 6864 ♦ fax: 250 383 6804
email: info@trafford.com

The United Kingdom & Europe
phone: +44 (0)1865 722 113 ♦ local rate: 0845 230 9601
facsimile: +44 (0)1865 722 868 ♦ email: info.uk@trafford.com

10 9 8 7 6 5 4 3 2

For Auntie Joyce

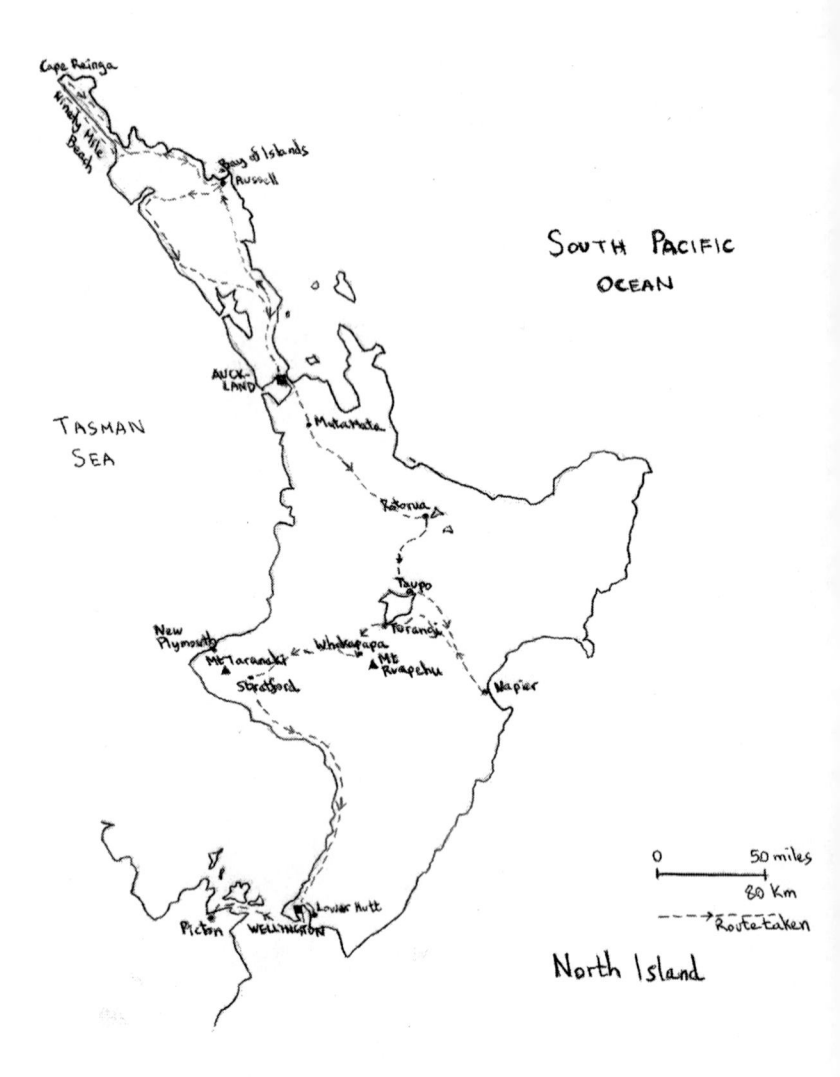

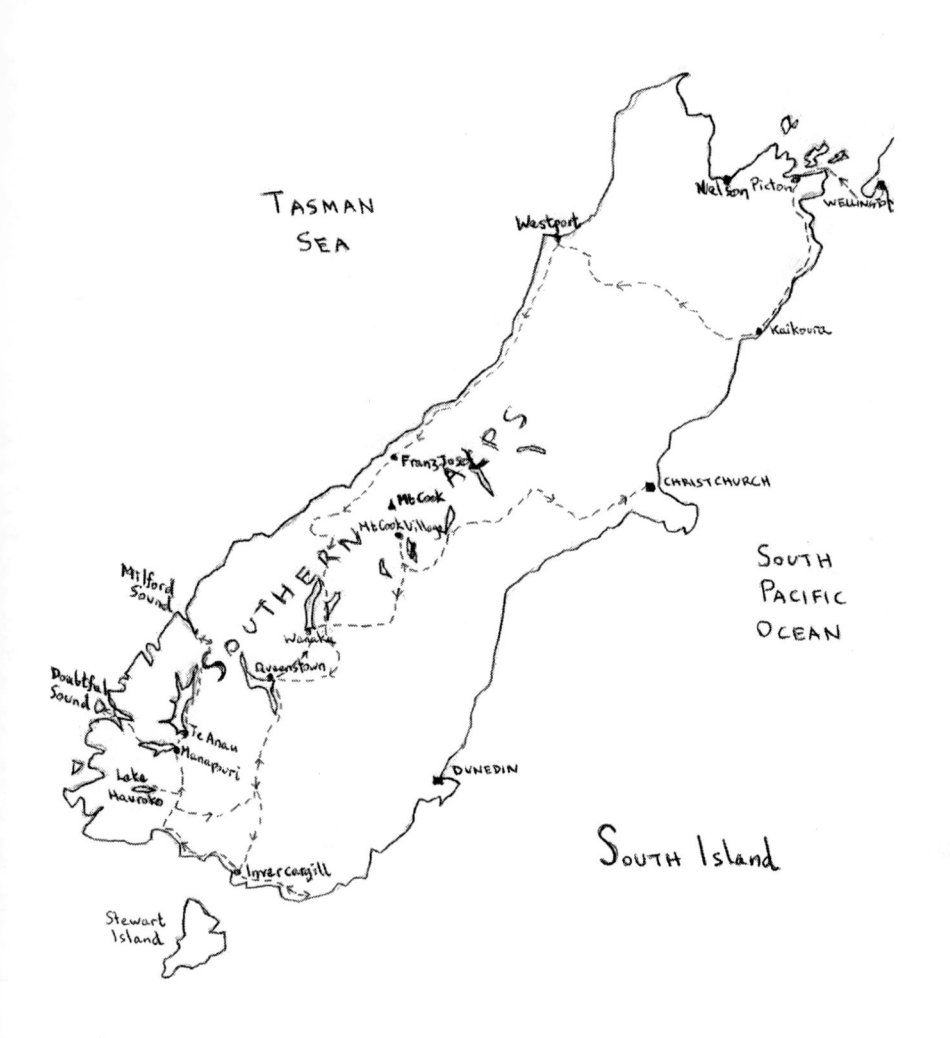

Contents

Introduction

(1) The Journey Begins
(2) The Winterless North
(3) Back on the Road
(4) Whakarewarewa
(5) To the Mountain
(6) The Forgotten World Highway
(7) Snowdrops in August!
(8) The Case of the Disappearing Whales
(9) Coast to Coast
(10) South to Franz Josef
(11) Running Away
(12) Sailing Westwards
(13) Milford Deep
(14) Pigeon Day
(15) Return to Queenstown
(16) The 1255 Steps

Epilogue

Introduction

"Trolling around New Zealand" the young immigration official had written on the reason for visit section of my landing card. This level of informality even by officialdom was indicative of what was to come and I could tell I was going to like this country. Finishing a flight of epic proportions which had given us intimate knowledge of the airports of Dubai, Singapore and Brisbane, Jacqui and I finally stood in our last airport – Auckland, New Zealand. It seemed much more than a couple of nights back when I'd ceremonially thrown my last packet of cigarettes in the bin at Manchester. I wondered, could I stay a non smoker? The next few days or rather the next hour or so would tell. Emirates had fed us well and what we both needed first was some fresh air and exercise!

Why New Zealand then? Well it has always been somewhere on my list of places to go since we'd nearly moved here when I'd been about 7 years old. Dad had been offered a job and was ready to go and I'd voted in favour, having found out that they had real volcanoes here – in such a way are the decisions of 7 year old boys made – but Mum had said no at the eleventh hour – too far from the relatives.

I'd seen one of those holiday programmes a year or so back where some guy had done a trip in North Island by camper van and it had looked like a good way to see the country. That along with watching one of my favourite episodes of "Ray Mears Extreme Survival" which sees the intrepid explorer going to Fiordland and Mount Cook, kind of re-established New Zealand on my "places to go next" list.

The previous year I'd met Jacqui and it turned out that she wanted to come here as well, though with her being a teacher we'd had to come in July/August which is the Southern winter. The up-side of this was that we got a really good deal on the camper van. We'd paid about NZ$1000 or about £400/US$700 for a rental totalling 31 days not including pick up and drop off days. Once we realised we could actually afford it we had begun planning the trip more seriously though our planned route was never set in stone. The idea had been to plan a general route that would take us to most of the places we wanted to see but which could be altered if necessary, once we had started the trip.

So here we were at last, stood outside arrivals at Auckland airport waiting for the man from Apollo to bring us our van. Yes – they even pick you up from the airport. There's something I like about starting a trip – whatever plans you've made, you still never quite know where you'll end up.

Chapter One
The Journey Begins

Indicating left, I turned the small van that was to be our home for the next month into Mount Eden Road and headed towards downtown Auckland. The sun shone warmly through the windscreen as we passed the row of shops where a bored looking dog appeared to be considering whether to wander into the road or not. The weather matched my mood and my co-conspirator and future wife, Jacqui, to my left looked as happy as I felt. It was a great feeling to be away at last after all the months of planning, though we had enjoyed our couple of days in Auckland.

We'd stayed the last 3 nights at Jacqui's friend Nicola's house in the leafy suburb of Three Kings. The Three Kings incidentally were not gift bearers from the East but 3 water towers built on the hill behind us that used to be visible around the area. I say, used to, because only the largest one known as the Big King remains, the walk to it giving great views of Auckland. Jacqui had known Nicola for years and having emigrated to New Zealand she'd kindly invited us to stay when she knew we were coming out here.

"Here's where we turn" said Jacqui from the navigator's seat. We'd reached the fashionable district of Mount Eden with its bars and restaurants lining the road. Turning here avoided the city centre and led us around towards the waterfront and a ring road that would take us to the main route north out of Auckland. The traffic became busier here for a while but in a surprisingly short time we'd negotiated the city without getting lost and were heading over the Harbour Bridge, the gateway to Northland.

Our plan was to go first to the Bay of Islands and do a boat trip to the famous "Hole in the Rock", then head up to Cape Reinga and Ninety Mile Beach before returning past Auckland to Rotorua. This was the centre of Maori culture in North Island and is also where the thermal springs and geysers can be seen. We then intended to go to Tongariro National Park with its three volcanoes including North Island's highest peak Mount Ruapehu, where I hoped to climb one of the peaks and Jacqui planned to go skiing. Next we planned to visit Wellington, the capital city before crossing to South Island. In the South we planned to go first to Kaikoura, the home of the whale watch trips then cross the South Island and Southern Alps to travel down the wild and rugged Tasman Sea coast in the west, visiting Franz Josef Glacier. We hoped to do a flight here over Mount Cook and its glaciers. We then envisaged continuing to the self styled adventure capital Queenstown, famous for inventing the bungee jump – Jacqui "Definitely not", me, "We'll see when we get there" was the verdict on a bungee. If we survived Queenstown we wanted to go to Invercargill and Bluff at the Southern most point of South Island with the possibility of a trip to Stewart Island before heading for our joint highlight, Fiordland, where we both wanted to sail up Doubtful and Milford Sounds. The pictures we'd seen of these places were, in Kiwi phraseology, "totally awesome!" The deal with the campervan was that having picked it up in Auckland we could drop it off in Christchurch before flying back to Auckland for our return flight to Manchester, in the U.K. This gave us the chance to go to Mount Cook village on the way back if we had time.

We realised of course that many things may be weather dependent especially those activities involving boats, aircraft or skiing and climbing, even more so as this was the Southern Winter. Travelling in July and August was necessary as Jacqui was a teacher. I, being self-employed could go whenever I liked as long as I could afford it but I don't get paid holidays! The weather so far had not been very wintry but this was the sub-tropical part of North Island with winter temperatures more like October in the U.K. We had also realised that even with nearly five weeks here we couldn't see everything and we were probably missing some good places – Coromandel, East Cape, Nelson and Dunedin to name a few but I think we'd planned a good itinerary that would take us to most of the places we both wanted to see.

The city was left behind now and along the roadside was farmland interspersed with evergreen forest, the strange looking tall eucalyptus trees standing out above the others and the fascinating deep greens of the tree fern rainforest occasionally pressing in towards the road. We reached another overtaking zone; there are lengths of dual carriageway every few miles along the highway allowing safe overtaking of slower vehicles, trucks, tractors etc. I was doing the speed limit but even so several cars raced past at 20 or 30 over the limit. There seems to be this obsession, yes I've done it myself as well, that you need to overtake a bus, van or lorry even if it isn't going particularly slowly. That's not just a Kiwi thing though; most U.K. drivers do the same. A more worrying trait in New Zealand was the apparent readiness by drivers to risk serious injury or death by overtaking on blind corners in between these bits of dual carriageway even though it was never far to the next one!

The road was now winding uphill and thick rainforest had appeared on both sides, huge ferns overhanging the road. Up we climbed until nearing the top of the pass a sign advertised a café and the "Dome lookout" which seemed to be some kind of viewpoint. Jacqui suggested stopping for lunch and changing drivers so I pulled in at the car park. There were only 2 or 3 cars there on what seemed to be the highest point of the road. The restaurant was open but we decided to investigate the Dome Lookout first. A sign-posted path led into the dense rainforest and zigzagged steeply uphill. We were both fascinated by the rainforest never having experienced it before. Well, apart from the day before when we'd driven from Nicola's to the Waitakere (pronounced Wai-takery) Range to the west of Auckland.

Waitakere had been recommended to us as a good day out from Auckland lying within easy reach to the west of the city. We'd driven first of all to the visitor centre with its wooden walkways above the forest canopy and fascinating Maori statues hand carved from whole tree trunks. After a good look round we'd continued on down to the Tasman coast at Piha beach for lunch. This had been an idyllic spot where the huge waves of the Tasman Sea crashed onto a long length of sandy beach overlooked at one end by the Lion Rock with its white stone statue of a Maori girl said to be awaiting her husband's return. Later in the afternoon we'd driven the narrow and winding forest roads to Karekare beach where the film "The Piano" had been shot. That had definitely been the kind of beach that we both like. Totally deserted and accessed by a forest path and hence unfrequented by the people who only go to the places they can drive to.

Behind the restaurant we followed the muddy trail up into the forest, at first steeply and then less so as we left the road behind in its dip. The path was clear enough though the trees closed in as we went further. Soon we were walking in a deep green twilight surrounded by the moss covered trunks of the huge tree ferns. An eerie silence prevailed broken only by the occasional noises of birds somewhere above in the canopy. The whole place brought to mind Tolkien's "Fanghorn" and seemed to harbour an ancient presence that was calm and peaceful rather than threatening. We walked, always uphill, for maybe half an hour in this half light world until all of a sudden bright sunshine appeared in front and the trail led out onto a small deck like structure above a clearing. In front the ground fell away steeply and we were greeted with a view over the forest and back down the range of hills in the direction of Auckland. The road was visible to the right and below us climbing the hillside opposite towards our start point.

Jacqui commented about a long tailed bird which was above us on the edge of the trees. She later identified it as a Fantail and it treated us to an amusing display of flying as it flitted with great agility between the moving branches of the forest edge and the open sunlit clearing. The sun had gone in again as we set off back, looking forward to some food at the restaurant. Indeed, as we emerged from the forest again at the bottom of the path, a few spots of rain were starting to fall and it was much cooler. Only just warm enough in fact to enjoy an outside lunch. One large burger later, we returned to the van where Jacqui took over the driving and I gave directions. It was easy enough as there only seemed to be one main road heading north.

Our next stop that afternoon was just outside the town of Whangerei (pronounced Fan-ger-ay – the "Wh" being pronounced as an "F" in the Maori place names), where we called in at a supermarket to buy food and essential supplies such as wine and beer for the next few days. It felt strange to go past the tobacco counter and not buy cigarettes. I'd given up at Manchester Airport 4 days ago and was surviving on Nicotine gum! "I'll have a gum in the van" I commented to Jacqui as we paid for the provisions. She was very pleased that I'd stopped, having never smoked, and that I'd managed not to buy any while we'd been here.

Another thing I'd noticed was that now we were out of Auckland the shops, especially the tills, counters and advertising posters resembled the shops I remembered going in as a kid maybe 25 or 30 years ago in the U.K. with everything looking strangely old fashioned. I'd read or heard somewhere that New Zealand was somewhat like the U.K. was 30 years previously. This must be one of the things that they meant. It was quite nostalgic and I liked it.

Back in the van and heading north again, I completely forgot to have that nicotine gum. Giving up had not been as bad as I thought it would have been, well so far so good. I'd long been part of that group of people you often see huddled in all weathers, like some secret society outside offices and shop doorways, but my last cigarette had been in the smoking room of Manchester airport after which I'd ceremoniously thrown the packet in the bin and bought the nicotine gum instead. Not that I was one of these people who could give up just like that. I'd spent the last six months cutting down, first of all waiting until after breakfast for my first one, then after lunch and finally going a full day without but smoking of an evening. This made it, I think, much easier to take the final plunge and a flight lasting over 24 hours plus stops was as good a time as any. The only times I'd really wanted to smoke were when we got off the plane and a few occasions later that evening. The gums took the edge off the "cravings" which actually didn't last more than a couple of minutes anyway. After the first day here, maybe 3 days after my last cigarette, any cravings to smoke became few and far between hence me forgetting the gum just now,

The car ferry from Opua to Okiato in the Bay of Islands region was one of those small flat pontoon-like boats similar to the one that we'd nearly fallen off on the way to the Isle of Skye on a family holiday years before. It was therefore with some trepidation that I sat in the cab of the van with Jacqui waiting to cross the half mile or so of water to the Russell road. Luckily the sea was calm in this inlet and the crossing passed without us or anyone else ending up in the water enabling us to drive the last couple of miles to Russell itself.

Russell is a delightful town, like something out of the 19th Century. The wooden buildings lining the single main street each have an individual character and the small harbour probably hasn't changed much in a hundred years. The town faces across the Bay of Islands to Pahia, a couple of miles away and is backed on the other side by the palms and evergreens of the sub-tropical forest. Our spot on the campsite couldn't have been better either, a level terrace in the trees with a view out across the bay below, the site itself consisting of wooded parkland sloping up behind the town.

After our first meal cooked in the van, we ventured off on a wander to explore a bit. A path led up behind Russell to a hilltop where there was a flagpole and an absolutely fantastic view over the whole of the Bay of Islands and out towards the Pacific Ocean. The weather was such that this view was enhanced further by the quality of the light. A rain shower was moving in towards us yet it was backlit by the sun which sparkled on the sea below the grey clouds. I called it my best "non mountain" view!

The flagpole itself had some history. Russell was one of the earliest, possibly even the earliest settlement of Europeans in New Zealand and there was the inevitable dispute between the local commandant and the Maori chief. This dispute manifested itself in the English putting up a flagpole and the Maoris coming along and chopping it down when no-one was looking. This went on for some time with even an iron clad pole succumbing to the axe until an agreement was finally reached leaving the present pole standing to this day. As the sun went down we left the glorious view and returned in gathering darkness to the van to enjoy a bottle of wine and a few games of cards before we were both too tired to play and had to put the bed down.

One gained entry to the living area of the van, which was separated by a curtain form the cab to keep the warmth in, by a sliding door on the left side. The cab area was to the left with the sink and gas cooker in front while to the right was the sitting area with the 2 seats facing each other across a table. This area converted into a bed in an operation reminiscent of one of the events from "It's a Knockout" or so it seemed after several glasses of the red stuff. The bed however was comfortable and after the long drive we both slept well on our first night away in the van. I even forget to have a nicotine gum, again!

Chapter Two
The Winterless North

We stood on the open deck aboard the cruiser edging slowly out from Russell Harbour. After a minute the skipper revved the powerful diesel engines and we rapidly picked up speed, heading out into the blue waters of the Bay of Islands. The weather was glorious after a chilly start and we were aboard a "Dolphin Discoveries" cruiser bound for the Hole in the Rock out in the South Pacific.

That morning had been one of relaxation and chilling out after jet lag and charging about had finally caught up with us both. We'd had a look around Russell and researched the various trips to go on from here. We'd opted for "Hole in the Rock" today and this company seemed to offer the most 'wildlife orientated' version of the trip. For tomorrow we'd booked, yes, a coach trip, to Ninety Mile beach and Cape Reinga. This was either really unusual as neither of us "do" coach trips, however the Fuller's trip was recommended by the campsite as they do the drive along Ninety Mile beach, which we weren't insured to do in the van. In addition it was a long way and would save us a lot of driving.

Over the loudspeaker, skipper was explaining our route and that though we stood a very good chance of seeing, and for those who chose to, swimming with, some of the Bay's Bottlenose Dolphin population, they were wild creatures and not circus performers so nothing was absolutely guaranteed.

We'd crossed the bay and slowed down to take a look at some of the seafront houses amongst the palm trees on the inner islands. Alright for some, hey!! Heading out again we soon made our first sighting of dolphins in the distance off the port bow. The skipper explained that we'd head over and see if they wanted to play. Apparently, like us, they're not always in the mood and will swim off if this is the case. These dolphins however were in the mood and soon came over to swim alongside our boat. They seem to do this purely for fun and enjoy being pushed along by the bow wave. I guess it's a bit like hitching a ride!

Now was the opportunity to swim with the dolphins. Maybe half of the people on board chose to do this but myself having the aquatic skills of an average sized house brick, decided to remain on board and dry. Jacqui also opted out though she was tempted. I was perfectly happy watching the dolphins from the boat as they were coming very close anyway. "If I was designed to go in the sea, I'd look like him there", I commented to Jacqui, pointing at a large bottlenose by the boat. The skipper explained that for those in the water to attract the dolphins it was best to move around and swim under the water as much as possible rather than hang about as they would soon tire of stationary swimmers.

This guy's commentary became hilarious once all the swimmers were in the water. After the initial inevitable comments about sharks, he launched into a tirade against the swimmers that would have put any school games master or army drill sergeant to shame!
"Come on you lot! Dolphins 'll be asleep at this rate!"
"Put yer back into it!"
Myself, Jacqui and a few of the other passengers were in stitches by now and he was clearly enjoying himself.
"They're off to play with the penguins now!"
One of the swimmers seemed to be heading away from the group towards another boat some 200 yards away.
"Wrong boat!" yelled the skipper through his loudspeaker.
"We're BEHIND YOU!"
"Oh, I give up!"
When all the swimmers were safely recovered from the sea we resumed our journey, a few of the dolphins swimming alongside the boat for a little way as if to guide us to the hole in the rock.

We came to the outermost islands of the bay and sailed through a channel between them and into the much rougher water of the open sea. Several miles in the distance a headland jutted out made of some very high rocks and cliffs. That's where we were headed following the distant coastline around. As we approached the headland it was revealed that the island off the coast was several hundred feet high and had a huge natural arch through it. This was the Hole in the Rock.

We passed the lighthouse above Cape Brett and carefully negotiated the passage through the arch. It was maybe 50 yards through to the other side and was an impressive sight from below. Much bigger than it looked from further out. On the return journey we slowed to view a seal colony on a large rock between Cape Brett and the Bay of Islands. These were New Zealand Fur Seals with whom we'd become more acquainted later in our journey. We didn't see any dolphins on the return journey but there was perhaps an explanation for this.

We passed a small boat on the way back which we learned was manned by a local scientist who was studying the Orcas or Killer Whales who occasionally entered the bay from the open sea. She'd radioed our skipper to say that Orcas had been sighted earlier. The dolphins would certainly stay out of their way. The remainder of the trip back to Russell was spent searching the sparkling waves for a sign of these huge marine predators. They too however, remained elusive.

That evening back at the van it had turned very calm and clear and hinted of frost which was uncommon up here at Bay of Islands. It did mean we needed to use the van's fan heater for the first time during our after-tea cards and wine session. Switching the heater on soon made the small living space too warm but when it was switched off it became instantly cold again. It was a case of fiddling with the thermostat until we achieved a happy medium, leaving it on a low setting seemed to be the knack to it.

We were though extremely pleased with our van. It was about the right size for 2 people and was almost luxury after the tent we were used to. We discussed the pros and cons of tent versus campervan versus caravan. That spring we'd been camping at Ardgarten in Scotland and had been 4 days in a small tent watching the rain continuously falling outside. Yes, we had stayed dry but only just! The response had been to buy a bigger tent but the issue still remained.

We'd seen these massive bus like vans with about sixty bikes and as many canoes strapped to the side but neither of us fancied the idea of manoeuvring one of those through country lanes and up and down hills.
"Imagine the fuel bills", I added to Jacqui.
No the van we had was about right. The only disadvantage we found was that once having parked up and plugged into an electric hook up, discovering you were out of milk or eggs for breakfast or much, much, worse, out of beer! You then had to pack everything up and disconnect from the power before driving to the shops. Ok, here in Russell that wasn't a problem as it was a short walk to town and the general store. The other option was the caravan. As children, our parents had both, first of all taken us camping and had eventually bought caravans. In my case this had been when Mum became fed up of sitting in a tent in Scotland in the rain. Funny that!!
The major advantage of a caravan is being able to park up and then go off in the car without having to pack up as though moving on every time you want a pint of milk. That was the option we ended up taking, becoming known as

"Tin tenters" to our camping friends. Warm, dry tin tenters, I will add!
Back in a small white campervan on a chilly July night in the Bay of Islands however, it was bedtime. We had a coach trip to join the next morning!

By torchlight we'd made our way from the van down to Russell Harbour to catch the first ferry of the morning, which left at 7.00am. Patches of fog hung atmospherically over the still water while the stars shone from a cold night sky. We were the only two people to board the ferry for the short trip across the bay and the dawn was just adding a blue twilight to the sky as we disembarked in Pahia. We crossed a much larger harbour area passing many small fishing boats and pleasure craft moored around the jetty before crossing the car park to join our bus.

The coach thankfully was about half full and there was plenty of room as we set off, stopping once more at a hotel just out of town to pick up a couple more people. Our driver and tour guide, who could have been a voice double for Sean Connery, began a well informed commentary of our route. I was just glad to be on the bus and out of the cold. Outside, the sky was lightening as we drove on a tree lined road similar to the one we'd driven up past the Dome lookout. Fog patches appeared in clearings and partly obscured the view of palm trees silhouetted against the dawn sky. Near a place called Keri Keri we passed several Kiwi fruit plantations. It seemed a little odd listening to 'James Bond' talking about kiwi fruit but it was interesting enough. I've eaten enough of the things in my time! Keri Keri it seemed was one of the main producers of New Zealand's 'national fruit' and they are grown on vine-like plants which are protected from the wind by tall hedges all but surrounding their fields.

Leaving Keri Keri behind we travelled northwards soon turning off the main road and heading more inland. We were heading for the Puketi Kauri forest, the massive trees used by the Maori in the past to build their war canoes from. Into rolling hill country, the sun was now up and shone on the white frosted grass from a cloudless blue sky. Our guide informed us that it was rare to get frost up here in the Winterless North, as the region north of Auckland is known, and it was indeed soon vanishing in the sun. The road plunged again into thick forest, this time of huge ancient trees rather than the now familiar tree ferns and palms. These were the Kauri. This forest had once extended much more widely but had been largely destroyed by early European settlers. Can't we go anywhere without wrecking *something*? We stopped in this wood for long enough to take a walk through the Kauri trees and to appreciate their immense scale. I've not been to America's giant redwood forests but I imagine those to be similar. Many of these trees were over 1000 years old.

On Northwards and leaving the Kauri forest behind, our bus took us past a spectacular view of the sea again at Doubtless Bay and on past the Keri Keri peninsula through almost completely flat farmland to our second stop off at the "Ancient Kauri" visitor centre. This place was so named because local farmers had discovered, buried beneath their fields, the perfectly preserved (but not fossilised) remains of a prehistoric Kauri forest which had once existed in this region. The trees had been carbon dated at up to 40 000 years old, yet the wood was preserved and still usable for carving. Apparently the lack of oxygen in the peaty ground had prevented the wood from decomposing in the normal way. All manner of carvings were available for sale here but the showpiece was a stairway actually made inside the massive tree trunk of one of the ancient trees leading to the upper floor. Quite fascinating! Coffee and a large sausage roll for a late breakfast and then we were off again. We were now heading for the famous Ninety Mile Beach. Our plan was to access the beach at the southern end and drive up to the north. The direction one did this was purely down to time and tides.

Heading through an area of grassy dunes we emerged onto a vast flat expanse of sand backed to the west by the endless rollers of the Tasman Sea. Ninety Mile beach is 60 miles long. Don't ask me! I don't know. Maybe someone got miles and kilometres mixed up or something. There is something vaguely surreal about hurtling along a sandy beach, just out of reach of the waves, in a luxury coach at 50mph. Jacqui was even more fascinated than me and kept the video camera on for the first 20 minutes.

The whole journey takes well over an hour but we stopped about three quarters of the way and we all got out to be greeted by the ever present sound of the ocean now the engine had stopped. The sun was warm and illuminated a light salty haze drifting in off the breaking waves. After a wander, we climbed a sand dune where Jacqui took a photo to give us an idea of the size of this place. The sand and breaking waves stretched interminably, as far as the eye could see in both directions. Behind the dunes was a wooded area, home to a herd of wild horses, though we didn't see them. Onwards once again! The exit from the Northern end of the beach is up a river. This was thankfully not too deep and the guide drove us safely through the water without getting stuck until we stopped as the foot of a massive sand dune. The river is I suspect why hire vehicles aren't allowed on the beach and I was glad we had come by bus. We were given the opportunity to borrow a surf board; climb the dune which was about 300 feet high and body board back down again. This was immense fun and I was amazed by the speeds that could be reached sliding down a sand dune!

We had our lunch at a delightful beach called Tapotupoto Bay before journey's end at Cape Reinga. We parked up and walked the last half mile or so along a precipitous headland to the lighthouse where a signpost informs you of the distances to various places around the world. On this clear blue cloudless day, the view was fantastic, extending across the constantly moving ocean to the Three Kings Islands in the north while to the east side is the wide sweep of Spirits Bay and to the west and south the rugged headland of Cape Maria Van Diemens with the distant dunes of Ninety Mile Beach and the crashing Tasman Sea beyond. Out along the jutting promontory beyond the lighthouse could be seen a lone tree outlined against the restless waves. This place is known as *Te Rerenga Wairua* and is sacred to the Maori as the final departure point of the spirits of the dead. Their souls are said to travel via the roots of this tree to a point on the Three Kings Islands where they view Aotearoa (New Zealand) for the last time before journeying to *Hawaiki* – the name for both the Underworld and the spiritual homeland of the Ancestors. We were now at the northern end of North Island and as far as we go in that direction. Our journey now would be southwards.

The long drive back to the Bay of Islands was uneventful this time being by road rather than along the beach and evening was drawing in by the time we reached Pahia. After a delicious meal of fish and chips and a walk along the darkening sea front we returned to the harbour for our ferry back across to sleepy Russell. Leaving the lights of Pahia reflected on the sea, we agreed that Russell had been a good place to stay. Pahia was nice but it was also bigger and busier. If you come in summer I'd imagine it to be something of a bustling seaside town. Russell, however, had a timeless charm about it. Maybe too quiet for some but I guess it's what you prefer.

Chapter Three
Back on the Road.

The petrol gauge in the van read nearly empty and the sign outside the only petrol station in Russell read "Closed". This was not a good combination of events.

We both remembered, however, that there were one maybe two petrol stations in Pahia which would be more likely to be open on a Sunday morning. A slight change of plan then, instead of heading down the coast road from Russell it was back to the car ferry and up the main road to Pahia where, indeed, our mini petrol crisis was solved.

The weather was still good and by 10:10am we were back on the road and heading south and west. The aim was to cross this part of North Island and head down the Tasman coast to Auckland, hopefully getting past Auckland and camping somewhere in the Hamilton area for the night. For a short while we joined the main highway heading back north again before turning off this to the west and following quiet country roads. The landscape was rural with farmland and forest interspersed with occasional small villages. The flatter country of the east became hillier as we headed towards the west coast and with the hills, the forest began to take over again.

After a somewhat longer distance than we'd expected, the road descended to a particularly beautiful section of coast along an inlet to our right. As we approached the point where this met the open sea, we found a 'viewing' signposted off the road so stopped for a walk. Passing some unusual rock formations a path led out to a headland overlooking the restless Tasman Sea. The wind was getting up from the northwest and the sky rapidly clouding over indicating the good weather we'd had was coming to an end.

On again, south, following the coast on our right. This area seemed almost deserted compared to the East coast around the Bay of Islands. The road, almost a single track in places, led on into the lush green hills along the coast. We met hardly any traffic along here and in the forest the huge Kauri trees became more evident. We stopped for lunch at the Waipoua Kauri forest home of the "King of the Forest" *Tane Mahuta*. We followed the walkway to this particular Kauri tree which is 2000 years old and about three times the size again as any of its neighbours.

Heading south downwards towards Dargaville and Jacqui was spotting Pukeko's by the roadside. These are a colourful type of wild hen native to New Zealand that inhabits fields and marshes. By now the rain had begun and it spattered on the windscreen as we rejoined the main Auckland road (the one we had left town for to go to Russell) as the evening approached. Here it became progressively busier as we approached the city and nightfall. Auckland is home to around a third of New Zealand's population and most of them seemed to be on the road that night resulting in the only major traffic jam we experienced on the whole trip. After crossing the harbour bridge once more the motorway through town became completely snarled up and as the driver I wanted a cigarette for the first time in ages. Nicotine gum however, did the job and was in fact the last one I had.

The jam had been caused by a crash further along and once clear of this we resisted the temptation to go back to Nicola's but carried on into the wet night heading south away from Auckland. By now we had both had enough but we seemed to be in an area devoid of campsites so it was decided that we would camp in one of the lay-byes off the main road. These seemed to be at regular intervals and consisted of a length of road maybe a quarter of a mile long running parallel to the main highway but shielded from it by thick bushes and trees. Pulling into the next one, eyes sore from the car headlights reflecting off the rain soaked road surface, I stopped the engine and we sat for a moment listening to the sound of the rain drumming lightly on the roof of the van. At least the 'site' was free!

We busied ourselves making and eating chilli and rice before settling down to an evening of wine and cards. The curtained rear window to my right was occasionally lit up as a car pulled in behind and then again as they left and passed us. The noise of a motorbike made me jump as it roared off into the night, I'd not seen it come into the lay-by. I was a little jumpy going to the toilet which was the hedge outside the van. The rain had stopped and a watery moon was shining through the clouds making eerie shapes in the trees and bushes. Behind the hedge there just appeared to be open fields, no lights at all were showing. I told myself to stop being silly. New Zealand has one of the lowest crime rates in the world and plenty of people camp in lay-byes. There were no axe wielding serial killers about! Returning to the warmth and light of the van we had a last game of cards and I finished my glass of wine before settling down for the night. I soon went off to an uneasy sleep and a dream of shadowy highwaymen stalking the Auckland road seated on thunderous black motorbikes.....

Awoken by the morning sun through a gap in the curtains of the van we were both soon up and making bacon butties for breakfast. Through the open side door of the van we were greeted by a view of endless sunlit green pasture dotted with grazing cows. Here was a scene straight out of those ads for Anchor butter, for this was the dairy region of North Island. It all looked and felt very different to last night in the dark and the rain. Revitalised by breakfast and the sun, we were on our way again by 9:15am.

We were heading towards Rotorua with the intention of stopping at a town called Matamata which was one of the film locations fro "Lord of the Rings", where we'd have some lunch and look at the film set if they were open. The country here was all farmland, flat with no forest and the road was pretty much straight as I sat in the passenger seat. The drone of the engine was beginning to make me nod off but then a sign caught my eye. It was quite clearly advertising "Pony Poo" for sale! Now I don't know whether

"Pony Poo" was better for the garden than any other kind, but it was a dollar a bag if anyone's interested! Amused I spent the next ten minutes looking fro other strange things for sale from the farms on the Matamata road but that was the only one of note.

On arrival in Matamata we found a car park and had a wander up the busy main street dodging occasional light rain showers. We found the tourist information and booked on a trip to the "Lord of the Rings" location for 10:45am. First of all though was a disaster on the camera front. Jacqui is a keen photographer and her camera had at that moment decided to give up the ghost and cease all co-operation. After an expensive trip to a camera shop, made less traumatic by the fact that she'd been looking to upgrade the camera soon anyway, we grabbed a coffee in Subway and boarded the bus for "Hobbiton"!

We arrived at the film set which was a few miles from town on a farm owned by the Alexander family and were given a fascinating tour of the site by a guide who clearly loved her job, and I don't blame her! We were told all about the efforts that had gone into finding the location and then keeping it a secret while filming was going on. If you stood overlooking "Hobbiton" there was no sign of human influence on the land around, apparently this was one of the deciding factors. We were told that the film company had agreed to return the set to its original state after filming had finished but heavy rain had prevented contractors from doing most of the demolition work. By the time the ground had dried out enough to resume, people had discovered the location and a steady stream of visitors were coming to see the site. The Alexander's, enterprisingly decided it was better to leave the hobbit holes and village there. I had massively enjoyed both Tolkien's book and Peter Jackson's film trilogy so it was really interesting to have a look around. I'd recommend it to anyone passing through this area. It was quite poignant to walk down the path from "Bag End" out of Hobbiton and to rejoin our own journey. Well, after a steak, pepper and lettuce sandwich from Subway in town!

    The afternoon was spent driving down to Rotorua and looking for a campsite. The town itself was quite busy and built up and the whole place smelt of sulphur. This was due to the various thermal springs and vents all over town. You could be driving past a residential area then suddenly there'd be clouds of steam rising into the air from unseen holes in the Earth. We had internet print offs that we'd brought with us of various campsites listed around the country. Jacqui found one at a place called "Blue Lake" which looked good on the photograph, so we made for that one. It was off the main road and some distance out of town heading up into the hills, and back into the rain forest once again. The road climbed steeply uphill before crossing a small pass in the woods then running alongside a lake surrounded by thickly forested slopes. On the right was the campsite. "There it is", pointed out Jacqui.
"What a spot!" I replied.
"We're getting good at this" she retorted happily as I pulled into the site consisting of wooden cabins and a shop completely surrounded by native forest.

There weren't many people here so we booked in at the shop and parked in a bay which backed into the rainforest. These woods always made me think that there should be monkeys in the trees but in fact New Zealand owes its rich variety of bird life to the lack of large mammals or predators. After a walk part way around Blue Lake it was turning to dusk and was beginning to rain slightly so we settled down to a relaxing evening and planned the next day's trip and activities to the sound of the evening's forest birds around our camp.

Chapter Four
Whakarewarewa

I've travelled around the country of Wales quite extensively, living in Cheshire not so far from the border, and though I can't speak Welsh I think I've managed to master the pronunciation of most of their place names with a reasonable accuracy. The Signpost in front of me, however, was in a different league altogether, for here was a truly unpronounceable name. I was defeated!

The village of Whakarewarewa is a traditional Maori settlement just outside central Rotorua in the midst of an area of geothermal activity. The air smelt strongly of sulphur with clouds of steam billowing in the chill morning air and, waiting for our guide to show us around the place the air was full of the sound of bubbling water. Our guide was an immediately likeable 'grandmother' figure. She emanated both enthusiasm for their chosen way of life and at the same time a sadness that it was disappearing from many areas. Here at "Whaka" the people chose to live in the traditional way even using the boiling springs for everything from cooking to open air bathing. These tours, she explained, were a way of the village earning money to preserve this way of life.

The sounds and smells here had immediately brought to mind my visit to Iceland a couple of years previously so I was surprised when our guide began to talk about Iceland. She knew all about Geysir (which is where our word "Geyser" comes from) and went on to explain that Geysir and Whaka were somehow linked. Incredible maybe, but each time new cracks had appeared in the rocks here, there had been renewed volcanic activity in Iceland.

We were shown around the village and then to the two geysers "Pohuta" and "Prince of Wales Feathers" on the edge of the village which erupted in spectacular fashion. The run off from the geysers entered a large pool maintaining it at a temperature of a heated swimming pool much to the joy of the village children. She then informed us that there would be a display of traditional dance in the village hall so to meet her again outside the hall in about 40 minutes. We duly wandered of among the wooden buildings of the village admiring the intricate carvings of the meeting house in the centre. Many tours of this kind would have shepherded us around but not so here. People were just getting on with their normal lives oblivious to us gawping tourists.

I think everyone there thoroughly enjoyed the dance show in the hall including the performers who were also accomplished singers and musicians. There were only a dozen or so in the audience this being out of the main tourist season, but I got the impression they did this show regardless of the audience sizes to keep up the tradition and stay in practice. The highlight, of course, was the Haka, as performed by probably the best rugby team in the world, the All Blacks to strike terror into the hearts of their opponents before matches.

Leaving the hall after the show there was a sudden change of mood. Our guide had re-joined us looking very distressed and explained apologetically that she had to leave the tour and could we look around ourselves. A family member (all villagers were classed as family members) had sadly died following a long illness and she had to go to the main meeting house or "Hangi" to help take care of the arrangements. Our hearts went out to her and no-one really knew quite what to say other than she must go immediately to be with her family and how sorry we were to hear the news. On that sad note ended a most enlightening tour of "Whakarewarewa" although I still couldn't pronounce the name properly. Jacqui and I drifted away from the group, some of whom were going in search of lunch and after a brief look at the boiling mud pools which resembled large pans of porridge, headed back to the van outside the village.

The plan for the rest of the day was to head for Taupo on the shore of North Island's largest lake, Lake Taupo. We set off intending to stop and look at another thermal region, the Waimangu Volcanic Valley, about 30km south of Rotorua. The Waimangu Valley was formed on 10 June 1886 during a major eruption of the nearby volcano Mount Tarawera. The eruption destroyed the then famous Pink and White terraces to be seen in paintings at the visitor centre, and re-shaped the entire region. After a tasty lunch at the visitor centre, we embarked on the walk around the site. We were out about one and half hours in all and our route led firstly, past a wooded crater on the right - all vegetation here by the way has grown back since the eruption, it was all destroyed at the time. From there we passed a simply awesome lake called the "Frying Pan "lake. This feature is close to 200 metres across and is covered with clouds of steam. To add to this eerie effect the water constantly bubbles and hisses as gases rise to the surface. It's warm too; the lake temperature is 55 degrees C and pure acid.

We followed the trail leading up to the left through the trees called the Mt Hazzard trail which led past a near boiling lake of deep blue colouring under its blanket of steam, Inferno Crater Lake, much smaller than the first one. The path led steeply uphill before emerging at a viewpoint where the 1100m Mt Tarawera was visible across Lake Rotmahana. From this point we descended back down in a loop to follow the steaming river back up its valley towards Frying Pan Lake which is its birthplace. The leaflet available from the visitor centre is very informative, giving a full history of events of the site. Apparently between 1900 and 1904, the world's largest geyser was active here, erupting to an amazing height of 400m! The whole area was fascinating but it was time to move on and back in the van we continued our journey southwards.

Driving towards Taupo we began to get distant glimpses of a high snow capped peak in the south. This would be Mt Ruapehu at 2797m, the highest point on North

Island. Before we arrived in Taupo, we stopped the van just off the main road leading through pine forests to view the Huka falls. While not the highest falls in New Zealand they are certainly some of the most spectacular, being the main outflow from the dam at Lake Taupo. A huge volume of water crashes down and into the rapids below the dams following a deep gorge-like channel with pine forests on both sides. A scene more reminiscent of Scotland or the Alps than the scenery we'd been used to so far.

Heading into Taupo reminded me even more of the Alps, Lake Geneva to be precise. The town sloped down to a long lake front similar to those along Lake Geneva. Lake Taupo is massive, almost like the sea and far away across its blue surface were the snowy summits of the Ruapehu region. It was possible to make out the two peaks of Ruapehu and Ngauruhoe with the lower flat top of Mt Tongariro in front of them. It was almost like a different country, yes being in Europe again. Gone were the tropical looking tree ferns but with the change, the weather had turned much colder. I enjoyed a delicious curry while Jacqui had venison, in a cosy lake front restaurant with a view of the sunset on the snow of the distant Ruapehu behind me out of the window, across the lake.

We camped at the Taupo Top Ten holiday park back up the hill from town and got back to grips with the van's heating as it was a clear and frosty night here. I did notice as well that I hadn't had a nicotine gum for some days. I hadn't even thought about them. Did this mean I was now a non-smoker? That evening we made use of some of the sites facilities namely the laundrette.

The following morning we headed off to see Napier for the day. Napier is famous as the "Art Deco Town" and it is fascinating place to visit. The town was almost completely destroyed by an earthquake in the early 1930's and was rebuilt in the style of the day. A good job they made of it too! Why they couldn't have done something similar to Britain's war damaged cities, I don't know. What did we get? Concrete monstrosities!

It was like entering a time warp, visiting Napier and a very pleasant experience. We would probably have camped there had we known what it was like. Driving back to the Taupo region we followed the bank of the lake road to the southern end nearer to the mountains, though they were now hidden by intervening ridges, arriving that evening in Turangi on the lake's southern shore. We stocked up at a supermarket and found a campsite in amongst the trees within walking distance of the town. Turangi was different again. It was how I imagine small Canadian towns to be, mostly light wood built homes and shops full of fishing and outdoor gear.

It seemed to get dark early aided by a chilly mist off the lake and promised to be another cold one. We decided on an early night with a bottle of wine and cards rather than staying out and looking round the town which had been the earlier plan. Besides, in a small shop in the town which had

sold among other things dried meats and fishing rods we had discovered the future......
The future was Chocolate coated apricots!!

Chapter Five

To the Mountain

In the cold of morning not long after the sun's appearance over the eastern horizon we drove out of the campsite and onto the deserted street leading to the main road out of Turangi. Fog patches hung over the town and lakeshore and it seemed that the whole world was still asleep. We left town on the main road heading towards the National Park and began a steady climb, steepening into bends as we reached the wooded slopes leading out of the valley.

Jacqui had found a leaflet for a company called "Mountain Air" who was based on the way to Whakapapa, our destination for today. We thought we'd call in on the way and book a trip as they advertised very reasonably priced flights over the volcanoes. Stopping at a 'viewing' which was in a forest clearing to the right of the road the exceptional clarity of the day became apparent. The ground dropped away in front revealing Turangi, still partially mist shrouded, and the vast blue expanse of Lake Taupo several hundred feet below shining in the clear atmosphere. There was not a cloud in the sky and the view extended to Taupo and beyond on the far side of the lake.

Another camper van was parked here and by the sounds and smells of cooking coming from the open window I think they'd spent the night up here. Not a bad spot, definitely preferable to the side of the Auckland Highway! Continuing through the woods we stopped again, this time on the shores of a lake called Lake Rotoaira. My map showed us to be at 573m over 200m above Lake Taupo yet it was much warmer here on the wooded shore, the calm surface reflecting the blue of the sky. There was silence here apart from the occasional cry of a bird and opposite, a few miles distant rose the snow topped peak of Mount Tongariro at 1961m the nearest of the three volcanoes in the park, clouds of steam rising ominously from a vent in its the lower slopes.

Moving on again the road gradually climbed higher, leaving the trees behind and emerging into the 'tussock' country, an open plateau like region of big skies and rough windswept grasslands though there was no wind to speak of today. As we drove round the side of Tongariro, the middle of the 3 peaks, the 2287m high, Mt Ngauruhoe slid into view its conical shape making it instantly recognisable as a volcano. Snow covered the top of half of Ngauruhoe ("Mount Doom" to Lord of the Rings fans) and seemingly most of the huge bulk of Ruapehu which had appeared further on in the distance, their white tops shining in the bright sunlight. To give an idea how clear the air was, in the other direction across intervening lowlands stood the snowy cone of Mt Taranaki, 2518m, North Island's second highest peak, 120km to the west.

Presently we arrived at the airstrip and pulled into the car park. The strip itself had been levelled into the surrounding tussock country and a couple of single engined planes were parked near the office end of the runway. A helicopter noisily came into land behind the building as we went in. As their prices were not too expensive and the weather so good, we opted for the longer trip that took us over all three volcanoes. We went up to the desk to book the trip and hoping we could go that day.
"We can go in about 10 minutes if you like," said the cheerful young guy behind the desk.
"Sounds good to me, "I replied, surprised we could go so soon.
"Well, no time like the present, weather's just perfect too," he added. He disappeared for a minute into another room before returning wearing a coat and carrying a set of keys. We followed him out of the door and round to the nearest of the planes, a single engine Cessna. Five minutes later I was in the seat to the right of the pilot and Jacqui was ensconced in the rear seat armed with camera and video recorder.

We bumped slowly at first then gathering speed down the grassy airstrip. All of a sudden the bumping eased then stopped altogether. We were airborne. The tussock grasslands slowly fell away and the scale of this area quickly became apparent. The road leading in a straight line towards Whakapapa was revealed heading off at right angles from the main road we had travelled up. Communicating through headphones because of the roar of the engine, our pilot pointed out features below as we gained height in a series of wide climbing turns. The main road was now a thin grey ribbon heading back towards the blue of Lake Taupo while the slopes of Tongariro loomed close by.

After taking what seemed to be ages to get up here, we quickly passed over the first 2 volcanoes, Tongariro with its frozen crater lake and the steep sided Ngauruhoe, which the pilot explained was "quiet" today. Sometimes clouds of steam rose form its crater but nothing today. Still going up we headed for the higher Mt Ruapehu. The air in the cabin grew thin as the altimeter passed 10 000 feet and we flew over the last volcano. The Crater Lake at the top of Ruapehu was not frozen but steamed in the cold air. You could probably see most of North Island from up here and we did two circuits of the mountain also viewing the ski areas, before the pilot throttled back the engine for the long descent back to the airfield, landing just over 30 minutes after take-off.

Whakapapa is the highest village in New Zealand situated approximately 1100m above sea level at the northern base of Mt Ruapehu and to the south of Mt Ngauruhoe. After our amazing flight we'd driven up the road to Whakapapa village and booked onto the Department of Conservation campsite here. These sites are government owned and have usually basic facilities with cheap prices to match. They are also situated in some of the best scenic areas of the country. Somewhat disturbingly there were signs everywhere instructing people where to meet i.e. in what direction to run, in the event of the volcano sirens going off! Apparently the most immediate danger here was that of "Lahars" or mud flows which can sweep down the mountain from the Crater Lake even in a relatively minor eruption. Fortunately, the mountain is well monitored and people should receive plenty of warning if an eruption were imminent. The notices gave the current risk level as "low" and our ability to run was not put to the test during our stay here.

I'd decided while we were here that it would be good to get out walking in the mountains. Jacqui also wanted to have a day skiing as it was a good while since she'd been and Whakapapa had a reputation as one of New Zealand's best ski resorts. The most famous walk in this region must be the Tongariro Crossing but this seemed a long route for winter with the short days and snow cover higher up. I'd opted for the highest trip on North Island, the Ruapehu Crater climb. This route climbs a point known as "The Dome" to the north of Crater Lake and reaches a height of 2672m. Though not a long route, it was reckoned to be a serious undertaking in winter so I'd need to go with a local guide or I'd be having ski lessons tomorrow!

I found a number for a guide in the visitor centre in the village which was also equipped with an interesting exhibition on the area. I rang the guide but he was out. Deciding to try later we had a drive up the 'Bruce Road' to the ski area. The car park at the 'Top of the Bruce' was just above the snow line at about 1600m. The ski runs seemed busy but not crowded and the nursery slope off to the left was devoid of any obstacles to hit such as trees which boded well if I ended up learning to ski tomorrow instead of ascending the white summit which towered overhead. Escaping the cold, we hopped back in the van and headed back down for lunch in Whakapapa before driving over to the start of the Tongariro Crossing. We had a walk along the path here for about half an hour each way, just as far as the first hut on the route, the Mangatepopo which is a wooden structure set on the tussock land below Mt Tongariro and Ngauruhoe.

The weather seemed to be holding with the skies clearing again as the sun got lower in the west. The temperature was already below freezing as we walked from the van down to Tussock Bar on the main street of the village where we had a delicious pizza and a couple of beers. I phoned the guide again whose name was Paul and who said he'd be pleased to do the crater climb the following day on account of the weather being spot on for it. I needed to confirm by phone in the morning though. We had a last beer and a short walk in the cold, pausing to admire the clarity of the unfamiliar southern constellations in the clear night sky before retiring to our house on wheels for the night.

We were both contented and pleased with our trip so far. This place Whakapapa was even better that we'd expected. Everything in the village within walking distance and the fantastic scenery – it could so easily have poured with rain as had frequently happened on trips to Scotland

and The Lakes for both of us previously. Auckland and Bay of Islands had both been fantastic and the Rotorua area interesting but up here was the highlight so far. After tomorrow's activities we planned to head for Taranaki via the mysteriously named "Forgotten World Highway" though we both worried unduly that the van's insurance didn't cover us for driving on so called 'unsealed roads' which are basically dirt tracks, this route containing 20 or 30 miles of them. After this we'd head to Wellington before crossing to South Island.

Friday 5th August dawned clear and sunny and having confirmed, the guide Paul picked me up by the camp shop just after 8am. We set off to pick up ice-axe, crampons and avalanche safety kit from the hire shop while Jacqui drove our van up to the ski fields. I got on with Paul pretty much immediately with his laid back attitude and enthusiasm for the mountains. We drove up to the Top of the Bruce and boarded the ski chairlift to take us to the top station at just over 2000m. It soon became apparent that my climbing companion was enigmatically known as "The Doctor" to pretty much everyone we talked to on the way up. I never did get an explanation of this other than that he wasn't a medical doctor but the name had 'kind of caught on'. I'd look out for the "Tardis" in the village when we got down!

Leaving the top chairlift station at 2020m I had a quick lesson how to use the avalanche locator beacons we both carried before we began the rather risky business of crossing the upper ski runs leading to the open mountainside above.

Snow and weather conditions were perfect; the sun was shining from a clear blue sky with visibility over 100 miles from this height. This also meant there were a fair few people hurtling at great speed down the mountain on planks of wood some of whom appeared to have little control of where they were going.

We survived crossing the ski runs in an operation akin to crossing the M6 motorway on roller skates thanks to the icy pistes and set off up the steep slope which was the start of Restful Ridge, the route we would follow up to the summit. It was possible to kick steps up the slope so crampons were not needed, though Paul led the way and did more of the work than me. Stopping for an early lunch roughly level with the top of Mt Ngauruhoe across the valley we both took some photos of the amazing view. Mt Taranaki was clearly visible as were the plains stretching for over 100 miles to the North. Between us and Taranaki, far below there appeared to be forested valleys where white layers of fog still lingered. This was the mysterious region of the Forgotten World Highway where we'd be heading tomorrow. Paul explained that even in summer we'd be lucky to get a day as clear as this.

The angle of the slope eased as we continued up Restful Ridge though I became a little breathless from the altitude as we approached the top. Here we followed the slope around with a deep snowy valley in the mountainside to our right. Edging up to the left, traversing the slope we emerged on the ridge top which narrowed sharply at a dip. There was no difficulty, though it would have been tricky had the snow been hard or icy, and we passed the dip as the ridge began to climb steadily upwards at an easy angle. On the right the slope fell to the valley which was sloping up to meet us as we progressed and to our left was a steep drop to a flat plateau.

All of a sudden we emerged on the snowy rounded summit. Below in front was the steaming Crater Lake I had seen the day before from the aeroplane, the snow running right down to it's shore and on its far side, only a little above us, the highest point of the crater rim with its steep icy rocks making it a difficult proposition. Beyond, most of the North Island was laid out below us. The view to the east took in more ranges of mountains well below us but holding small amounts of snow and fading to the distance somewhere near Napier. Behind, a layer of cloud had drifted in just below us obscuring part of the view.

I had been warm walking up but now the air was chilly, well below freezing in fact, though the lake below apparently stayed at around 25 degrees centigrade heated from below by vents in the volcano. Descending the ridge slightly to the South, past the summit we found a novel use for the avalanche shovels. Sitting on a shovel, the handle pointing forwards enables one to hurtle down a snow slope at some considerable speed, controlling one's descent with the handle. It is imperative however, bearing in mind the position of the shovel in relation to your anatomy, not to hit anything! Luckily the slope was smooth and the descent collision free and half a minute brought us down two or three hundred feet to the flat surface of the glacier which was the plateau we'd seen from the ridge.

Crossing the glacier led us to a gap in the crater rim overlooking Whakapapa and we made a swift descent of the slopes leading down to the top of the upper ski runs which we descended by shovel at probably over 30mph, keeping pace with some of the skiers. Paul was clearly practised at this and I caught him up near the top chairlift station having gone into the deep snow edging the piste 2 or 3 times before getting the hang of it. I don't know what the skiers thought of these two nutters going down the hill on their backsides but it was loads of fun and probably a lot easier to control than using 2 planks of wood as a mode of transport! I thought of some of my other mammoth descents; Colorado's Quandary Peak on a bin liner; the Aiguille du Tour and Galdhopiggen on my backside and now Ruapehu on a shovel. No, I guess it wasn't the skiers and boarders who were nutters after all!

Back In the bar at "Top of the Bruce" we met up with Jacqui who'd finished skiing a bit earlier and the 3 of us had a beer before Paul set off home and Jacqui and I drove our home back down below the snowline to the Whakapapa campsite. That evening it was back to Tussock's Bar for tea and a beer of course with Jacqui stopping outside the imposing Grand Chateau Hotel to photograph the sunset on Ruapehu and Ngauruhoe. She had enjoyed her day skiing and was especially pleased that she hadn't lost the knack after not going for a couple of years.

We both felt we could have stayed here a little longer but we had plenty more places to see and we'd probably come back to New Zealand at some point anyway. I'd like to come back here in the summer and maybe do the Tongariro crossing but for now we looked forward to our next day travelling.

Chapter Six
The Forgotten World Highway.

Saturday morning saw us finishing our bacon butties before unplugging the electric and driving out of Whakapapa village down the long straight descent to the main road. Turning left in front of the airfield took us presently to another crossroads. Left went to Okahune on the other side of the mountain but our route led in the other direction past National Park Village towards Taumarunui. The road made a gradual descent from the high country through a region of woods then sparsely populated farmland before descending into a broad green river valley over which hung banks of morning mist.

We headed roughly north for something over half an hour along the almost traffic free road, occasionally heading into fog, sometimes through green sunlit meadows. This must have been the river valley I'd seen from up on the mountain yesterday. The road now turned and began to head in a more westerly direction coming into the small town of Taumarunui. There didn't seem to be many people about for a Saturday morning even in town and we were soon through and following the road towards Stratford.

We were back in the in the rolling farmland once again and it was turning into a sunny day as the fog patches cleared. One thing I liked about driving in New Zealand was that on most roads there was very little traffic, plus they drive on the left like us! This road was quiet even by Kiwi standards and the farms and houses became few and far between the further we went. Forest began to take over from the farmland until soon we were following a single track lane through thick woods.

The Forgotten World Highway was a good name for this road we both agreed as the road became a rough dirt track winding through the forest. I was aware of the rule about not driving the van on certain unsealed roads but the condition of this one was generally good and I'd have been quite happy to drive my own car along it. At a steady 20 mph we followed the river as it wound through a spectacular wooded gorge. Stopping briefly by a riverside clearing, we found ourselves surrounded by an eerie silence as though the forest itself was listening. There was timelessness about this place almost as though the outside world wasn't there any more. Back to the reality of the van and the road alternated between paved and dirt track for maybe an hour before we began to climb up out of the almost claustrophobic stillness of the gorge. The forest became patchier and the odd farm appeared again but this was still very remote country.

Presently the road climbed up and down over several steep sided ridges. At the top of one these was a café called Kaieto where we stopped for lunch. The place was called

Tahora Saddle and we had a great view through the large windows back to distant Ruapehu as we enjoyed our lunch in the restaurant. It was a region of steep ridges and gullies with forest in the lower parts. I think the landscape was formed by water erosion rather than volcanic activity. We had a short walk outside up to a viewpoint where there was a helicopter landing pad. We seemed midway between Ruapehu and Taranaki which dominated the horizons in either direction. Before heading off I had to answer a call of nature. The outside lavatory was up some steps onto a veranda at the side of the building and had a large window facing the west. Thus I was able to enjoy a vista of endless green hills topped by Mt Taranaki whilst sitting in state. A loo with a view indeed!

The weather had turned much milder since leaving the high country of Whakapapa and the sun shone warmly for most of the afternoon as we headed west towards the snowy cone of Taranaki which loomed ever higher in front resembling Japan's Mount Fuji. Our gradual return to civilisation led us through the numerous farming communities centred on the town of Stratford in Taranaki province. Here we found a campsite just off the main street set behind pleasant suburbs. We booked on and set up only to realise a trip to the supermarket was in order. Back to the old debate of campervan, caravan or tent, with a tent or caravan everything could be left set up and it was just a case of driving to the shops. Here we had to unplug electricity, turn off the gas cylinder and pack away our coffee making things which did ensure that we kept the cooking area tidy.

It was no great hardship though, I doubt very much whether one could easily tow a caravan along the roads we'd travelled today and the weather later that night made a good case against tents.

After stocking up, we drove up the road leading to Mt Taranaki to have a closer look. The road led up through dense forest on the slopes to a viewpoint and car park on the side of the mountain, a great height above the patchwork of fields – about 1000m I think it was. We had a good view back to Ruapehu which disappeared in cloud as we watched. A cold wind blew up here and the weather was rapidly changing. The area is infamous for unsettled conditions and as the rain started on the way back I decided against climbing this peak the next day. We settled in to a wet evening back at Stratford the noise of the rain on the van continuing well into the night, a soft drumming that was strangely relaxing, sending us both off to sleep, assisted by the wine we'd picked up at the supermarket earlier.

Dawn brought in a grey damp "Scottish" kind of a day. The cloud was right down over Mt Taranaki and the night's rainwater hung in large drops from the leaves of the site's trees and hedges. We had decided, due to the weather, to get some miles done and head to Wellington today instead of the other plan which had been to go to the Egmont National Park which had looked pretty interesting. As if to vindicate this decision, a light rain started up again as we turned right onto Stratford's Main Street heading out of the town.

Eltham, Hawera, Patea .... the place names rolled past. At least the rain had stopped again as we followed the main road for Wellington. I was contemplating cow populations as we passed field after field of the creatures. The sea could be seen off to the right at times but the view was generally a pastoral one. Still on the agricultural theme, we stopped for petrol at the town of Bulls before a lunch stop at a lay-by maybe 20 miles further on. Finally in the late afternoon over 200 miles after leaving Stratford we followed a section of motorway along Wellington Harbour exiting at Lower Hutt where there was a campsite. It was in a semi-industrial area, one of the few we'd seen, but the site itself had good facilities and was populated, rather amazingly, by a large group of ducks which had an uncanny knack of appearing outside the van's open door whenever either of us cooked anything to eat. They seemed to know everyone's meal time and could be seen going from van to van in hope of a free feed.

Whether or not the ducks would have appreciated my chilli I'm not so sure. At the supermarket the day before Jacqui had bought me a bottle of sauce to add to my portions and leave out of hers. The small bottle left the user in no doubt as to the contents. It was emblazoned simply with a picture of a bright red chilli pepper and in red letters the single word "Fire"!

After a very spicy chilli and rice we headed off to the beach for an evening walk. Despite being a built up location, we had an enjoyable walk to a jetty which we wandered out along to where a couple of fishermen were attempting to catch their tea. As the sunset faded out into the lights of Wellington across the bay we wandered back in growing darkness. Tomorrow would be our last day in North Island before we flew home and we'd be catching the ferry on Tuesday across to Picton on South Island.

Chapter Seven
Snow drops in August!

I awoke to the sound of birds – the incessant quaking of ducks in fact – right outside the van. Momentarily confused I then remembered where we were. The people in the van next to us must have been having an early breakfast. Looking at the clock it wasn't actually all that early but not to worry, there was no rush. Eating breakfast, while the sites resident population of aquatic birds gathered expectantly by the van, we decided on what to do that day. The plan was to get the bus into Wellington that afternoon and find somewhere to have tea there. The bus would save us finding somewhere to park and it stopped just 5 minutes walk from the site anyway, before lunch though we decided to head off to Kaitoke Regional Park a few miles outside Wellington.

We drove up into the hills just outside of town and parked up before having a walk through a deep wooded valley, following the river to yet another "Rings" site. This was where they'd used as a location for Rivendell though unlike Matamata, nothing remained of the set. It was a good spot though with thick native bush clinging to the steep sides of the gorge and growing right down to overhang the river. A good walk and it was back to the site for an early lunch followed by a bus ride into Wellington. The bus took us into Lower Hutt which had a good shopping centre – if you're into that kind thing – before following the coastline towards Wellington city centre passing the Inter-islander ferry port on the left which was where we'd cross to South Island tomorrow. The road ran in a more or less straight line parallel to the railway with the sea to the left and a wooded suburbia rising to the right as we approached the Kiwi capital.

What struck me about Wellington was how small it seemed for a capital city. Admittedly we didn't see the whole of the town but that was the impression we got walking through the centre. It had a vibrancy that you see in London or Paris but on a much smaller scale and that was a good thing I say. We were able to go on foot around most of the centre, following Lambton Quay, the main shopping area and passing the impressive looking Parliament building known as "The Beehive" for its distinctive shape. Apart from the area close to the harbour, the whole city seemed to be built on a hillside at the top of which was the observatory and the Botanic Garden. To get up here we used the Wellington cable car which is similar to the funicular railways seen in Switzerland. The present system was indeed Swiss designed though a tramway has run here since 1902 amazingly.

The cable car journey took us from the bustle of downtown Wellington's offices and shops swiftly to the relative calm of the parkland in which was situated the

Botanic garden and Observatory. There were impressive views from here down over the town and harbour area to the sea and across the bay to Lower Hutt and Eastbourne further around with its distant mountains beyond. We walked around a loop trail which took us on a tour of the Botanic gardens before returning us to the Observatory. Here Jacqui commented with incredulity "Snowdrops – in August! That's ridiculous. You can't have snowdrops in August! They're a spring flower". As today was the 8th August, the presence of the small white flowers seemed to indicate that, here in Wellington at least, August was the month for snowdrops.

From the Upland Road Station near the Observatory, we walked down past the suburbs just below the gardens which contained several very individual looking houses, some of a neo-Spanish type design and all with expansive views over the city and harbour. This seemed the place to live in Wellington. From here the streets sloped back down to the far end of the shopping area where Jacqui found the inevitable camera shop. This time it was to put the photos taken so far onto a disc to free up space on the camera. By the end of this trip we'll have been in every photo shop in New Zealand!

It was getting near teatime when we collected the photos so we began to look for a good place to get some food. Heading towards the harbour we passed a large museum and theatre and found ourselves on the waterfront area where, like in Auckland there was a choice of several bars and restaurants that had been converted from the harbour front warehouses. After the obligatory sea food and a beer we watched as a large number of people piled into a not so large boat which proceeded to speed off out of the harbour and across the bay. This turned out to be the ferry across to the far side – Lower Hutt and Eastbourne and this was how they travelled to and from work instead of using the bus. I later learned that the boat called not far from where we were camped. For us though it was the bus back which we found in a row of bus stops not far from the 'Beehive'. It was getting dark now and the streets were full of evening rush hour commuters reminding us that we were in the capital after all.

Back at the van and we had something of a chill out evening, not having to cook tea and wash up so we just planned where we'd be going tomorrow. The idea was up at 7am to get to the ferry terminal which we knew wasn't far, and then to make our way from Picton on South Island to Kaikoura. This was of course known for the Whale Watch trips, one of which we hoped to go on.

It seemed strange to be taking the van on a boat journey and leaving North Island. New Zealand's South Island was, from what we'd heard and seen on the internet and in our guidebooks, the island of wilderness and adventure so we both naturally felt excited about going there but we had been to some fantastic places already. From the "Winterless North" to the snows of Ruapehu and from Auckland to Wellington we almost felt at home here now!

Auckland had been our first experience of this country and on our first full day here, we'd left the van in Three Kings and walked into town, the day before we'd done our day trip to Waitakere. The city, being home to a third of the New Zealand population is larger than Wellington with much more extensive residential areas. Our experience though was only of the area from Three Kings to the city centre. We'd headed towards the Sky Tower which is the tallest building (at the time of writing) in the Southern Hemisphere and which dominates the whole of Auckland.

Once at Sky Tower which is pretty much central, we took the lift up for a bird's eye view of Auckland. Known as the "City of Sails" it's easy to see why from here. The harbour is full of small boats and yachts of all sizes. Apparently there are more boats per capita here than anywhere else in the world.

There's a choice of activities to be had at the Sky Tower. One is the "Sky jump" where from the roof of the lower observation deck you hurl yourself, lemming style, towards the street over 600 feet below. You wear a specialist jumping suit attached to a wire which slows your earthwards plummet to a gentle landing when you reach the street level. The one I opted to do was the "Vertigo Climb" to the "Crows nest" near the top of the radio mast crowning the structure. I'd booked on the trip and was introduced to the guide who showed me how to use the safety harness and ascender unit. I seemed to be only one on this particular trip even Jacqui opting out and we set off to the upper observation deck. Here we were collared by an elderly woman and her husband who'd spotted our harnesses.

"Are you jumpers then?" she enquired.

"No, we're climbers" the guide replied. She looked back at her husband, a look of puzzlement on her face before turning to us once again.

"What is it you climb?" she asked in a deliberate manner.

"The radio mast on top of here," the guide replied cheerfully.

"Oh" she said, looking form us out of the window to where a jumper was preparing for the quick way down back to us again and then to her husband before they both hurried off wordlessly. They clearly thought the place was inhabited by complete nutters! How right they were!

We exited the upper observation deck via a hatch in the roof from where a ladder disappeared up inside the hollow mast. Clipping the ascender onto a wire rope that would have held the weight of an elephant - could an elephant be persuaded to come up here of course - we began the ascent stopping for a rest mid-way. The ascender was a metal jumar-like device which could be pushed up the wire but not down so if you did fall off the ladder, you wouldn't go very far. After about 200 feet of climbing which took some effort up the vertical ladders we reached a door in the side of the structure. The guide opened the door and we stepped out into bright sunlight. The floor of the crows nest structure was one of those wire mesh types you can see right through and was separated from the streets of Auckland by a thousand feet of air. Now I absolutely love places like this but it was very easy to see how it came to be called the "Vertigo Climb"! The whole of the city was spread out below us and far beyond the harbour, we could see across to the Coromandel Coast and the distant Great Barrier Island out in the Pacific.

Re-united with Jacqui who would have hated every minute of the climb, not being a fan of see through metal floors and ladders, we'd set off down to the harbour area for a drink in one of the many bars. Auckland harbour, like Wellington, had a profusion of eateries but the harbour itself had more pleasure craft than Wellington's more business like counterpart. Rain had begun to fall as we enjoyed a drink by the harbour and so after a look around a few of the shops we had caught an early evening bus back to Three Kings.

We'd be returning to Auckland anyway on account of the fact that that's where our flight home to England left from.

Unless of course…….. Well there's an idea!

Chapter Eight
The Case of the Disappearing Whales

The tune of REM's "Leaving New York" played somewhere on a radio, the sound drifting across the breezy deck as the Inter-islander ferry "Arahuna" made her way out of Wellington harbour. The song was quite poignant as I looked back along the wake of the ship at the buildings of Wellington, lining the shore. Okay, this wasn't New York but we were finally leaving North Island and heading south. We'd packed up at 7:30am on a damp dewy morning and driven the 2 or 3 miles to the ferry terminal where we'd waited in line to board, driving onto the ferry then grabbing something to eat before the queues formed in the food hall.

The sun was climbing into a sky of azure clarity as the city of Wellington receded astern, the sea a darker blue than the sky becoming choppier as we headed out into the bay. The Inter-islander is the ferry linking the 2 main islands of New Zealand and goes from Wellington on North Island to Picton on the South Island. The voyage takes 3 hours and heads south east of Wellington harbour losing sight of the city when you round a headland. The ferry then proceeds roughly North West across the Cook Strait before entering the Queen Charlotte Sound reaching Picton at the end of this inlet. Strangely enough, Picton in the South is slightly North of Wellington. The size of the ship and the whole checking in procedure made this seem more like an international crossing than an internal one reminding me of the cross channel or North Sea Ferries back home.

Crossing Cook Strait a chilly wind blew but we were still able to comfortably sit outside - we both always insist on being on deck on ship when the weather allows it – in an area of deck protected by glass windbreaks. The sun continued to shine brightly showing up patches of snow, the first we'd seen since Taranaki, on the mountains of South Island which rose in a jagged line on the western horizon.

North Island began to sink on the horizon behind as we reached the entrance to Queen Charlotte Sound. Now began the most spectacular part of this sea journey. The blue waters of the sound sparkled in the sun and became surrounded by steep wooded hills rising into the clear air. In places the passage narrowed and then opened out again in a profusion of islands, bays and hidden inlets that reminded me of the coast of Norway between Bergen and Stavanger. Apart from a few boats and the odd shoreline cabin, there was little sign of human interference in this area and it looked worthy of future exploration. On reaching Picton which was tiny compared to Wellington, we left the ferry to drive up a winding hill road leading to the main highway where we turned towards Blenheim and Christchurch.

This was again like being in a different country. The roads were quiet and settlements few and far between compared to the North. The first town of any size we came to was Blenheim which had a frontier feel about it, very different to Wellington and Lower Hutt that we'd left that morning. Heading on, the railway following the road, we were in a rolling dry looking region of grasslands split by huge river beds which were overlooked to the West and South by the now cloud topped mountains. The other way, glimpses of the sea were caught from time to time.

Crossing a bridge of wooden construction extending several hundred yards across one of the river beds, a goods train passed going the other way. This was the main line heading between Auckland and Wellington on North Island and continuing in the South from Picton to Christchurch. It was, we later found out, the only route with a regular passenger service. Apparently the railway had been privatised years before and most services scrapped – sounds familiar!

Heading southwards, the mountains marched nearer to the sea forcing the road into a narrow strip overlooking the Pacific, the peaks rising steeply on the right into grey cloud. Rain had begun to fall gusting in from a grey and stormy looking ocean just below us. This was the first stormy weather we'd had and reminded us that we'd left the sub-tropical North behind. Stopping for a rest, photos and to change drivers I pulled into a roadside lay-by. Donning waterproofs we braved the weather to walk down a path where a viewing was indicated. The coast was wild indeed here, the road clinging to the sides of the steep mountains that dropped in rugged cliffs and headlands into the Pacific where the waves crashed, ending their journey of thousands of miles. Some where across there was the coast of Chile, probably as wild as this one?

"Look there's a seal" I shouted to Jacqui who was already getting the camera out.

"And another," as I spotted another on a rock just above the waves and...

"There's millions of them!" as I realised that a large area of the stony beach below was occupied by the large grey sleepy sea creatures otherwise known as New Zealand fur seals.

"That'll be why, "Jacqui replied, camera in hand, waving at the large sign behind, which said that Ohua where we'd stopped was a seal colony. Yes that would explain the presence of so many seals on the beach. OK, then not millions but maybe a hundred or so.

They were mainly sleeping or pretending to sleep but over near the edge of the surf was a large rock pool where six or seven baby seals splashed around out of reach of the huge waves and watched over diligently by one of the adults. The resting seals were getting a break from the kids and we wondered if they took turns at being 'nanny' guarding the crèche.

On through the rain and Jacqui drove the last few miles to Kaikoura where we left the main road and headed down a lane to the village. This was a delightful spot despite the weather with the single main street of mainly wood built cottages and cafes ending by the beach itself, the village reminded me a little of Russell at the Bay of Islands. We checked in at the campsite which was a walkable distance from the village and just over the railway from where

"Whale Watch" was situated on the coast. This was of course our first port of call though we were not surprised to learn that trips had been cancelled that day due to the weather. It doesn't unduly bother the whales; it's more the stomachs of the people in the boat that are adversely affected by these rough seas.

Booking on a trip for a quarter past one the following day we set off back to the village to deal with priority number two – food! This was a delicious meal of fish and chips for me and mussel chowder – a kind of soup – for Jacqui at "The Craypot" one of the café /restaurants in the main street. After our early tea, we drove out to the headland which is a magnificent stretch of unspoilt coastline jutting out into the Pacific from the main east coast of South Island. At a viewing here, a sign declares the view back along the coast to the Kaikoura Ranges, to be one of the finest views to be had anywhere in New Zealand. Peering through the wind blown rain at the mist shrouded coastline below where the mountains should have been, we agreed that it could be anywhere in Scotland or Wales and that it may be a good idea to come back in better weather.

There is another seal colony here and the enterprising occupants have made the discovery of great benefit to the comfort of seal-kind that grass is decidedly softer than boulders. The animals have hauled themselves past the rocky beach and lie spread out on the open grass and under bushes right up to the car park. They probably are even fed by visitors though that is discouraged as chicken nuggets and scraps of beef-burger are probably not best suited to their diet. The weather remaining stubbornly cold and wet, we didn't go far but returned to the campsite for a relaxing evening looking forward to the Whale watch trip the next day. The site was quiet and all that could be heard was the sound of the sea and the drumming of rain on the roof that became more intermittent as the night went on.

Wednesday 10th August dawned clear and frosty, the sun lighting up a magnificent vista of snow covered peaks, the seaward Kaikoura Range, which rose over 8000 feet above the coast. We had a walk into town looking round a few shops and visiting an internet café, these seemed to be a popular facility in South Island, finally heading over to the "Whale watch" centre excited at our trip. The sea had calmed down, the rain had stopped and visibility was now perfect so we were both, Jacqui especially, really disappointed to be told that the trip wouldn't be running because the whales had now gone missing.

The reason why Kaikoura is one of those places where sea life, dolphins and seals as well as various types of whale proliferate is due to the ocean currents here. Cold water from the Antarctic meets warm water from further North of here and the mixing, aided by a deep ocean trench not far off the coast creates an abundance of plankton and krill, which are the main diet of many species of whale. These whales therefore, notably the sperm whales for which the area is known, can stay in the same place without the need for lengthy migration, hence they can usually be seen year round. "Usually" being the operative word as nothing in viewing wildlife is absolutely guaranteed though "Whale watch" said they refund most of the trips cost if you don't see a whale which pretty confident. Today it appeared they had just moved further away from the coast than where they normally feed. We were told, however that, they would be running a trip at 7.15am the next morning as it was a good possibility that the whales would return overnight.

Booking on this trip cheered Jacqui up somewhat though our trip would be the one to see if the whales had returned. They ran the first trip of the day regardless, weather permitting and if no whales were seen, a spotter plane would head out to have a look. If that proved to be of no avail, the following trips that day would be cancelled. Disappointment over, we headed back to the seal colony at the end of the peninsula. We decided now that the weather had improved, to walk from the car park to the very end of the headland where there was no road. Passing the viewing again and looking back along the coast, the crashing waves and sparkling blue sea backed by snow covered peaks, yes the inscription on the sign had a point after all.

The path led up steeply to the top of the cliffs and across farmland until the end of the peninsula was reached. From here you could see on southwards down the coast where the main road continued its journey towards Christchurch still many miles off. Closer at hand was a small harbour area a couple of miles down the coast. This it turned out was where we'd sail from tomorrow. We didn't meet anyone else on the walk though we saw a few below on the beach who'd walked up round from the other side of the peninsula from near the harbour area.

Back at the car park we made a brew in the van, one of the advantages of a campervan, and watched an extremely large seal emerge from the sea and make his way to a rock in the middle of the beach where he took up residence. We called him "King Seal" and presumed he was the dominant male of the colony. He obviously wanted to appear big and hard so didn't join the easy life brigade on the grass. Some of the other seals were virtually sat in the car park today. Maybe they planned to hitch a ride into town to one of the seafood restaurants instead of heading out to fish the cold waters of the Pacific Ocean!

That evening was clear and starry as we set the alarm for the unearthly hour of 6am for tomorrow's trip. I hoped that we'd get to see a whale as for Jacqui it was the thing she'd most looked forward to on the whole trip.

Chapter Nine
Coast to Coast.

Awakening in the cold of dawn we had breakfast and packed up the van for that day's journey, which would take us from coast to coast over to Westport by the Tasman Sea. Outside the frost lay thick on the grass and the pale white peaks of the Kaikoura Range became tinged with warm orange as the sun emerged, the clear sky promising a fine morning.

Before any journey though we had whales to look for and excited at the prospect drove the short distance to the Whale watch centre. We were greeted by a spectacular dawn sky as out over the ocean banks of high cloud glowed various shades of red and orange in the light of the rising sun. After a quick briefing on what to look out for and the sea-life that inhabited this coast, everyone on the trip boarded a bus that took us round to the small harbour on the far side of the headland that we'd seen from yesterday's walk.

The boat was a large power craft similar to that we'd been in at the Bay of Islands only this time, like everyone else, we remained in side the cabin on account of it still being freezing outside. We were treated to a most informative commentary by a guy whose second job was probably as Kaikoura's resident stand-up comedian. Apparently the boat was packed full of just about every electronic device known to aid the search for the whales and once located one of the crew would look out for the small jet of spray from the whale's blowhole when they surface to breathe.

Most fascinating of the gadgets was the depth indicator. As we headed out into the Pacific it dropped suddenly from the region of 20 -30 metres to over 800 metres indicating the deep underwater trench just off shore where the whales and other creatures usually fed. They soon picked up the right signals on the sonar and headed at speed towards their source. When the boat slowed and began to drift on the ocean swell we left the cabin and went up top to look out. Almost right away we saw wandering albatross and Cape petrels. The albatross are amazing birds and it was the first time I'd seen one. With a wingspan of around 3 metres or 10 feet they glide effortlessly almost skimming the sea surface.

The whale had failed to appear, presumably it had dived again but they got another sonar signal and that time we were lucky. A sperm whale of approximately 60 feet in length was on the surface where it remained for several minutes breathing while our cameras clicked and video's did whatever video's do. There was something amazing about being in the presence of such a large creature. It could see us, being close by, but didn't seem at all perturbed by us being there. Slowly the whale prepared to dive. One extra large breath and it began to move forwards, the cameras on board all trying for that classic shot of the tail in the air before the creature's return to the depths.

We began to move to where there'd been another signal much to the relief of my stomach which hadn't enjoyed sitting there going up and down with the swell. I don't usually suffer from seasickness, I'm generally okay even if it's rough, but the slow up and down regular movement doesn't agree with me. A bit like theme parks, I'll enjoy the most violent high speed roller coaster ride but feel ill on a kid's roundabout!

There were no whales at the new site though we did spot a couple of seals, probably from the seal colony on the headland and more albatross which seemed quite common out here. Our skipper headed back to where we'd seen the whale as it was 20 minutes since he'd gone down and would be due to resurface again any minute. Sure enough we saw again, what was almost certainly the same whale. When he'd dived a second time, as there were not many signals on the sonar, we went closer in to the shore to look for the rare Hectors Dolphins which can sometimes be seen here. There are three main types of dolphin around New Zealand; the most common and largest is the bottlenose which we'd seen at Bay of Islands. Then there are the smaller Hectors and Dusky Dolphins. Unfortunately though, the Hectors were not playing today. At least we'd seen a whale and albatross which was a first for both of us.

Back to the port and the bus took us to the centre where we bought a couple of wildlife books before brewing up in the van overlooking the ocean outside the Whale watch centre. It was still only 9.30am and we'd already been on a trip out to sea! This was going to be a long day.

It was sad to leave Kaikoura as we both liked the place and decided to spend longer here if we came back to New Zealand. I drove our little van down the mostly empty road towards Christchurch for a few miles before turning off inland onto a totally empty minor road. We followed this for mile after mile without seeing a single car through a region of dry looking grassy hills. Distant mountain peaks occasionally showed themselves to the west and we discovered the original "one horse towns". The map would show a place name indicating the presence of a town or village but quite often there would turn out to be just a single house or farm or in some cases a petrol station. As we continued our travels through South Island's remoter reaches, some of these place names turned out to be uninhabited buildings with perhaps an abandoned car or two in the garden. It was these outposts of civilisation that spawned our theory that the real reason people had settled there was that they'd run out of petrol and were unable to leave. They were simply waiting for the day that someone else would come along and build a petrol station nearby. Then they would fill up their Morris Minors and Ford Anglia's and continue the journey to the shops they'd started years before. Well we thought it was a good theory but maybe we'd just spent too long cooped up in a campervan!

The road joined a more major looking road with the odd car and truck heading the other way as we approached Lewis Pass. Grey clouds had filled the sky during the course of the morning and these rested on the tops of serrated mountain peaks towering over the deep valley in which we travelled. We had reached the Southern Alps and what a fantastic area it looked for exploration, "But sadly, not today", I thought as we passed another side valley leading off to another range of mountains at its head. This was like the Scottish Highlands on a grand scale.

The road began a steady ascent of the valley side though it wasn't unduly steep and presently brought us to a more forested region. Here the mist was down and clung to the mountain above us. The rain began as we crossed the crest of the pass and the view disappeared as we entered the rain-soaked grey mist. Back in thick rainforest the road descended in a series of hairpin bends and emerged below the cloud by a spa/hotel which was the first habitation we'd seen for miles. Unanimously we agreed to go in here for lunch.

Looking at the grandness of the lobby area I was worried what the prices might be like but the menu was very reasonable. The place was surreal. Not just because it was in the middle of nowhere but it was all adorned in Japanese style with the large open restaurant area surrounded with oriental screens. Even most of the staff were Asian and to top it all we were the only customers on that damp winter's day. We opted for a chicken dumpling with noodles which was served in a large bowl and was absolutely delicious. A good call we agreed. The surreal bit returned halfway through the meal when, looking out of the half steamed up windows we observed a man who had clearly eaten a large number of pies, walk past wearing only a towel. Yes, pouring rain, only 5 degrees centigrade, towel weather of course! Then we saw the steam room where he was headed. There was a hot spring here and people came to bathe in the water. I still didn't fancy going out without my Gortex coat on though.

We changed drivers here and I took my place as navigator and passenger for the remainder of the journey to the Tasman. The rain battered the windscreen and dripped from the roadside trees as we headed – always downhill – away from the mountains. Presently we entered a series of wooded gorges ending with a town on the map which turned out to be an empty barn with the door missing. Reaching the level strip of land that is the west coast we turned right crossing a bridge over a wide fast flowing river and there was Westport.

Westport is a pleasant enough, if unremarkable, town of mainly wood built houses set out on a grid pattern which made it easy to find the campsite. There were small patches of rainforest or native bush as its known here, within the town's limits and the site was located in one of these. I noticed here that they had what were known as backpackers' accommodation. Some of the other sites had them but I hadn't taken the time to look closely before. They were basically a small one room wooden cabin with a bed and a cooker inside.

"What a great idea those are," I commented to Jacqui. We decided it would be the way forward, to look into building some of these in the Lake District or Scotland, although British planning rules, which seem to allow faceless corporations to destroy nature wherever they like, would probably object to providing a few budget huts for hikers and travellers who couldn't afford rip off hotel prices or million dollar 'lodges'. They'd be pretty handy whether you were hiking, cycling or even with a hire car. No tent to put up in the rain or van to pack up. Yes definitely much too sensible for UK planning officials. I challenge you to prove me wrong when I apply for permission!

The rain had stopped and we decided on a walk before it was dark. In Westport, the sound and smell of the sea was everywhere so we set off to find it. Through the largely deserted streets, where was everyone? We passed the wooden houses with their pristine gardens and into a lane through green fields where a bedraggled looking horse came over to investigate us. Another half a mile brought us to a deserted beach of tussock grass along an inlet which was the mouth of the river we'd crossed earlier. We'd crossed the country, for this rough water we now saw, was the Tasman Sea. Further out grey clouds gathered so we headed quickly back before the rain started up again.

Nowhere seemed to be open but luckily we had a bottle of wine we'd bought in Kaikoura and a couple of lagers were also discovered in the van. The evening was spent trying to work out the source of a noise on the van roof. We were under trees so we assumed a bird of some type but nocturnal ventures with a head-torch revealed nothing. The possibility of a possum was also considered as we read that these critters could climb trees. They were considered cute and cuddly in Australia but a "noxious pest" in New Zealand as seemed the case with many "introduced" or even non-native species. I don't think that the Aussies care much for the cute bunny rabbit though.

The rain that had been threatening finally arrived and put an end to our search for the mystery creature so we contented ourselves with scrabble, wine and cards accompanied by the sound of intermittent rain on the roof. Whatever had been up there clearly wanted to stay dry as it now appeared to have vanished.

Chapter Ten
South to Franz Josef

The "glorious twelfth", as its known in some parts of Scotland, dawned in true Scottish style – wet! It was though, much milder here than it had been in Kaikoura, we hadn't needed the heating in the van that night, and the rain did ease off as we drove out of Westport and over the bridge we'd crossed the day before.

We were heading south to the Franz Josef Glacier along the West Coast Highway, possibly one of the best drives in the world. I was amazed looking at the map to find that we were little more than 30 miles south of Wellington but we had a long journey today. The almost deserted highway crossed heath lands reminiscent of Bodmin Moor in Cornwall before gradually being swallowed up in dense unbroken native bush on both sides. The palms and the tree ferns had been almost absent on the Kaikoura side but they were back with a vengeance here. The weather too steadily improved, it was by now non-committal mistiness but the rain had at least stopped.

"Look there's one" Jacqui shouted and I had to brake to avoid a funny looking brownish red bird which was sprinting full pelt across the road in front.

"Saw it that time" I laughed back. It was a Weka and she'd spotted a couple since we'd left Westport. They were one of New Zealand's resident flightless bird population similar to a kiwi but the easier to spot not being nocturnal.

The road descended through the thick forest after some time and began to follow Westland's wild coastline. It was a fantastic coast, the deep green forested slopes reaching right down to the crashing waves of the Tasman Sea. Where there were gaps in the bush, the waves rolled up wide deserted beaches of golden sand. Inland the green hills rose into the clouds, the foothills of the Southern Alps. We'd made an early start, for us anyway, and by mid-morning we'd reached Punakaiki or Pancake Rocks, hardly seeing another car going either way. We'd been told in Auckland that this was one of the "must-see" places in South Island so we called in for a coffee at the tourist centre before going to look at the rocks themselves.

The whole coast here was comprised of stratified layers which actually did resemble stacks of pancakes formed into towers. It looked a kind of sandstone and had been eroded from a flooded cave below forming the famous blowholes. At high tide the pressure from waves below forces spray up into the air in spectacular fashion. Unfortunately high tide wasn't until later that afternoon but thanks to inclement weather in the Tasman Sea producing waves over 20 feet high, we were able to see some spray emerging from the blowholes, which became visibly more active even in the half hour we were there. Following the short trail around the strange rock formations, some of them eerily resembling figures staring out to sea, we made our way back to the van to continue our southwards journey.

A short way after Punakaiki the road climbed high above the sea and we stopped at a viewing to be greeted, in the car park, by another – rather well fed looking Weka and we decided these birds had an aura of cheekiness about them! Onwards again and presently to Greymouth, the first town of any size we'd seen since Westport. We stopped only for petrol as the plan was to reach Hokitika by lunchtime and it was now after 12. There was a rather interesting bridge in this area across one of the wide riverbeds intersecting the highway. The bridge carried both road and railway in the same single track width raising the worrying prospect of direct confrontation between our small campervan and a hundred tons of speeding diesel engine coming the other way. Luckily we survived the bridge without being smashed to a pulp having driven swiftly across and were able to reach Hokitika hungry but in one piece.

In actual fact although the railway ran the length of this coast and we saw some very impressive bridges over the rivers I don't recall seeing one train. Maybe they're an infrequent service as someone did tell us that the only regular trains were between the main cities. That would be shame as this coast would make a fantastic trip by rail.

We donned coats for the walk around Hokitika as the rain had started up again. This place had some character, like an old frontier town in a western movie. Half the shops sold

Jade and Gold but for Jacqui, the all important one was, yes, the photo shop. This having been located, we dodged the rain showers to go for lunch in a café before collecting the disc with the photos on. Our next port of call was Jacquie Grant's Eco World which we'd seen advertised as the National Kiwi centre. They had a fairly large aquarium as well as the kiwi enclosure which was in a dark room to mimic night time. The birds were pretty active; two even had a scrap while we were there, and they were larger than I'd expected. We'd wanted to come here, hence Hokitika as a lunch spot, as we know the birds are not easy to spot in the wild being nocturnal and extremely shy.

Returning into the bright daylight, the sun had come out between showers and was reflecting off the wet streets, we called into the "Jade Factory" where they had some very elaborate jade carvings and a couple of gold shops selling jewellery and real gold nuggets. I was quite interested in the information they had on gold mining in the area. The rivers of Westland were apparently rich in gold, I'd actually seen something about this, years before as well, but with the areas remoteness it was difficult to exploit to its full potential. This was really a good thing I thought, as large scale industry would spoil the region's outstanding beauty. A few small scale operations and individuals panning for gold wouldn't damage the scenery and eco-systems in the same way large scale industry would.

Jacqui and I had planned to get married in the near future and we had decided to try and find our wedding rings in New Zealand. We'd had a brief look in Wellington and we had another look here and though there were some nice rings here, we didn't spot "the ones". The plan was to have another look in Queenstown, though the wedding was nearly off when I declared my interest in spending several months here to live in a hut and pan for gold in the rivers of Southern Alps.

Leaving Hokitika via the supermarket we began the last stage of the drive for today. The sun had given up its battle with the rain clouds and the weather looked set in for the remainder of the day as the road left the coast and headed inland for the last stretch. The grey clouds clung to the mountainsides as we rolled into Franz Josef and booked onto a site called the Rainforest Retreat just out of town. The site was right in the woods and had excellent facilities. Despite the weather there seemed a lot more people here than at previous sites we'd been on, apart from maybe Wellington.

As evening arrived, we walked into town which was just one main street and had a really good pizza for tea at a big pub which was serving food. After a couple of beers we headed back to the van and had a couple more before turning in for the night. The rain continued unabated all night and was still drumming on the roof when we awoke.

After breakfast we decided to brave the elements and head back to town to investigate flights over Mount Cook and the nearby glaciers. This was of course weather dependent as under the present conditions nothing would be taking off from here. Even the birds were sheltering under trees!

We booked a flight with Glacier Southern Lakes Helicopters who offered the glacier landing option. I'd not been in a helicopter so it seemed a good opportunity, as a comparable flight would have been double the price in Europe. They seemed reasonably confident of going as the weather forecast was better for the next day. It had turned much colder but the rain still came down incessantly. Back to the site and we set off on a walk through the rainforest towards the glacier. We went for about an hour traversing steep sided hills but found our way blocked by a river which was much higher than normal, making a crossing unsafe so we returned to the van and drove up the road instead. From the road head was a short walk up to a viewing called Sentinel Rock which afforded us a good view of Franz Josef Glacier itself. The upper part was hidden in cloud but the huge river of ice, one of the few that has advanced in recent years, was clearly visible from here. One of the unusual things about this glacier and the neighbouring Fox Glacier, apart from their recent advance, is that they extend down to below 500 metres in a temperate zone. Glaciers at low levels are normally only seen much closer to the poles. An explanation for this, and the recent advance, could be that rainfall levels are so high here and given the high altitude of the mountains, over 3000 metres, that rain would fall as snow, rapidly building the glacier from above and causing it to move more quickly than most. If global warming caused increased rainfall, that would mean increased snowfall up on

Mount Cook, again speeding up the advance. A theory anyway!

    I cooked a chicken stir fry for tea before we went out again to watch a widescreen film being shown at the Alpine Adventure Centre on the main street. The film showed the region and the Southern Alps from the air and made us really hope for a change in the weather so our flight could go ahead tomorrow. We both must have been tired that night because we had an unused "2 for 1" beer voucher for the Monsoon Bar on the campsite! I wonder if they'd still let me use it if I go back any time soon?

Chapter Eleven
Running Away

I awoke to an unfamiliar calm. The rain which had drummed on the roof since we'd arrived in Franz Josef, had stopped. There was just the occasional defiant 'clunk' as drops of water from the trees above completed the last stretch of their journey earthwards. Jacqui was already up and had made a cup of coffee. When she saw I was awake she said with some excitement,

"Pete, get up and look outside! You can see mountains!"

The prospect of being able to see more of the Southern Alps than a wall of mist and rain soon had me out of bed and dressed, as did the prospect of our helicopter trip going ahead. Call me cynical but I hadn't believed for a moment that the weather would clear up.

Stepping out into the cold bright morning it had certainly done just that. OK, it was hardly shorts and t-shirt weather but there was a good chance of our flight going ahead. Where the grey sky had been, spectacular peaks towered into the blue, plastered with what looked like a huge amount of fresh snow. The snow line came down surprisingly low, almost to the valley itself and blanketed the treetops on the nearby hills. We walked up the road to the shops and went into the Glacier Southern Lakes office where we were told both good news and bad news. Yes, the flight would go ahead but not as far as Mount Cook which was still hidden in cloud. At least we'd get to do the glacier landing if the wind conditions were OK.

Crossing the road with the other couple who were on the flight with us, we headed down a side street to where the helipad was located. Once we were all strapped in and the doors secured, the machine lifted off. It was a different feeling to being in a plane or Micro-lite but just as brilliant. The ground fell quickly away and I was able to see beyond the village and over the huge flat expanse of the riverbed leading out towards the Tasman itself.

We were now flying over the forested slopes, the trees below and the noise of the rotors reminding me of the many Vietnam films I'd seen. As we gained height the trees became snow covered and we crossed several steep ridges soon climbing above the tree line. Now all below was rock and snow and finally a mass of snow covered ice as we reached the Fox Glacier. The light of the morning sun was dazzlingly reflected off the snowfields below us and the pilot pointed out Mount Cook in front, its high cold summit half obscured by ragged white clouds. We presently found a landing spot at approximately 2000 metres or 6500 feet on the upper part of the Fox Glacier, the wind from the rotors whipping up vast clouds of snow so a billion ice crystals glittered in the sun as we touched down.

Leaving the helicopter we discovered that the glacier was covered by a good 15 to 18 inches of fresh powder snow which had come down in the recent bad weather. The location of the landing was spot on with views of the nearby peaks of the Alps just above and down over the coastal mountains to the sea in the distance. It reminded me of when I'd been up Ruapehu earlier in the trip. That seemed so long ago now and I wanted to go climbing here too. The nearby mountains didn't look easy though and I would definitely need to come back in summer if I wanted to make any ascents. Back into the helicopter after taking photos and in another cloud of powder snow we set off again. This time we flew over the Fox Glacier before crossing a snowy ridge and a deep valley to reach Franz Josef Glacier. Now came possibly the most spectacular part of the flight.

We made several sweeping turns as we descended over the glacier flying seemingly close to the crevasses, seracs and tottering ice towers. In this way we, followed the glacier all the way down to the valley, flying over the viewing we'd visited yesterday before heading out over the ribbon like formations of the river bed. Turning over the river we made our return to the helipad for a smooth landing. Walking back to the van I think we both used every superlative there is in describing how brilliant the trip had been, but we needed to pack up now, as today we were going to Queenstown.

It seemed that we'd done the flight at just the right time because as we packed away the breakfast things and set off it clouded over again and once more threatened rain. We headed through the next village of Fox Glacier before journeying south on the mainly deserted highway towards the Haast Pass which would take us back over to the eastern side of the Southern Alps. For maybe a couple of hours we drove with the mountains on the left until mid-morning we stopped at Lake Moeraki where there was a walk through the rainforest to Munro Beach. This was the winter breeding site of a colony of Fiordland Penguins, although there was no sign of them when we got there. It was still a good walk though, we both loved these deserted beaches and this one you descended to through trees, hearing and then seeing the sea at the last moment. There was a profound sense of isolation and peace here as though we had just discovered the place. The resident penguins were apparently a shy breed and would hide in the tussock grass if people approached. They were probably there somewhere but we just couldn't see them. We reluctantly left the golden sands and crashing waves to venture back through the dark forest again not seeing a single person on the way back either. We had some sandwiches back at the van before moving on.

Light rain had started as we reached the Haast region, another area of mile wide riverbeds dominated by vast mountains. The road once again turned in land and began its steady climb over Haast pass, passing the spectacular waterfalls of Thunder Creek and Fantail Falls en route. Haast Pass isn't particularly high – only just over 500 metres but it's the southernmost main road crossing of the Alps and passes through some spectacular scenery. It was, however, high enough for there to be snow by the roadside as we neared the summit and once again that east – west division. At the top of the pass we left the rainforest abruptly behind and entered a treeless high country of tussock grass and wide horizons. The rain had been left behind as well and the winter sun shone on row after row of snow capped peaks stretching as far as the eye could see. The contrast with Westland's deep wooded valleys couldn't have been greater.

We stopped near the end of Lake Wanaka to take a few photos and walk down to the lake. If winter had been reluctant to take hold in Westland, it had done so here. An icy wind gusted down the lake and its wide valley ensuring we didn't stay out too long. Onwards we went over a minor pass beneath more towering peaks and so to the spectacular Lake Hawea. The road followed the western shore of this beautiful stretch of water for several miles before civilisation was once more reached. Leaving the lake and the high country behind, the wide but quiet highway descended into an agricultural region dotted with farms and small villages. We passed the turning for Wanaka which may have been a shorter route but we stuck to the main highway 6 as the sun began to dip towards the jagged line of mountains behind us.

The road followed a wide cultivated valley down past Cowburn where the highway number 8 headed off for Christchurch and dusk was beginning to fall as we followed the next junction towards Queenstown. Navigating was easy here and it wasn't long before we were heading back towards the mountains but further south. The Gibston highway – still number 6 – followed the Kawarau River Valley and crossed the gorge at the site of the Hackett

Bungy where people famously leap into the depths from the bridge attached by their feet to a giant elastic band. It was dark now though as we carried on and presently came to Frankton where we had details of a campsite at Kawarau Falls. The site was easy to find even in the dark and we drove in and went to book on, buying some wine and other supplies from the shop as we did so. The evening was cold and frosty but clear as we settled in for the night and the lights of Queenstown sparkled across the lake which was directly below our pitch. Another good spot we thought.

The morning sun revealed that we were indeed in a good spot. The site was built on terraces overlooking Lake Wakatipu with views across to what was actually the outskirts of Queenstown backed by snow capped Ben Lomond. I think a few of the mountains around here were named by expat Scots for there was also a Ben Nevis and a Ben Cruachan! We drove into Queenstown with the idea of looking for wedding rings before heading on to Invercargill. The plan was to come back here for longer on the way back to Christchurch.

I'm afraid that my first impressions of New Zealand's adventure capital were, shall we say, less than impressed. I do apologise to the good people of Queenstown if we caught the place on a bad day, but the streets were crammed with cars, the town centre parking was full and heading just out of the centre brought us to rows of half finished building sites with no space to park even on the side streets. The few metered spaces seemed to be limited to 1 hour which wouldn't give us long enough to have a good look around and shop for rings and when we'd seen about the fourth sign proclaiming "No Campervans " we'd had enough and decided "to go and spend our money in Invercargill instead". In foul moods we negotiated our way through the other cars that were also probably unable to find parking spaces and yes – we ran away!

Turning off through Frankton and crossing the river near last night's campsite we followed the road southwards, presently following the shore of Lake Wakatipu. Arriving in a quieter area calmed our moods down and we once again began to enjoy the journey through this region which looked exactly like Scotland. We decided that we'd probably over-reacted by running away but I suppose we'd been spoiled by empty highways and open spaces virtually since Wellington. The disappointment of not liking somewhere that was meant to be a highlight left a heavy feeling but we decided to go back and camp at one of the town centre campsites in Queenstown. That way we'd not have to drive around looking for parking that probably didn't exist.

The Scottish landscape of Southland rolled past outside, the hills bathed in sunlight, the air crystal clear and the road once again empty of all vehicles except our campervan, and that's the way it should be! The hills receded behind us and we travelled through farm country until we came to the outskirts of Invercargill where low wooden buildings led towards the town centre. Parking the van was completely hassle free and we set off, via Subway for lunch, to have a look around.

Continuing the Scottish theme, I spotted Tay, Forth, Spey and Dee on Invercargill's street names. There was plenty of information to be found at the Southland Museum and Art Gallery not far from where we parked. This revealed unsurprisingly that Scots had been the main early settlers to this part of New Zealand. We decided to try and book a trip to Stewart Island after abandoning Queenstown for the time being but despite the help of the girl at the internet café we were unable to get hold of anyone by phone or email. It seemed that although the places we'd been to so far stayed open for winter, Stewart Island didn't.

Visiting a couple of jewellers, we found a good selection of wedding rings we liked, at reasonable prices, and after some deliberation decided to take the plunge. We were pleased with our selections and it cheered us both up somewhat, especially Jacqui who'd been keen to go to Stewart Island to go on a Kiwi spotting trip. We could have got the ferry over there, but if everything was closed as it seemed to be, we'd be better to leave it.

We'd both liked Invercargill, the place can be characterised by the main dealership we'd passed on the way to the centre. Where most large towns would have a Mercedes Benz or Toyota, the huge showroom on Invercargill's main street proudly sported the sign John Deere, the rows of shiny brand new tractors lined up outside to tempt the populace of the rolling green acres surrounding the city. It was easy to find your way around too and people seemed to be more friendly and helpful than normal, so we decided to find a site here for the night. A return to the

Tourist Information at the museum on the way back to the van revealed that there was a site just off the main road the way we'd come into town. Before heading there though, we drove down the last stretch of road to Bluff where there was a signpost at Stirling point similar to the one at Cape Reinga, this one occupied by a lone seagull. The point is named after early settler William Stirling who founded Bluff in 1824.

It was a walk of about an hour with views across to Stewart Island all the way. When we returned to the van dusk was falling so we headed back through town and turned right off the main drag down a farm road where we came to the site. On the way there we'd called in at a supermarket to discover – disaster of disasters and on top of everything else – that the supermarkets in Invercargill didn't sell alcohol. The woman at the site however, who was as helpful as everyone else seemed to be in this town, came to our rescue by directing us to a "bottle store" only 10 minutes back into town.

As buying wedding rings was as good an excuse as we were likely to get we bought 2 good bottles of wine and polished them both off back at the site. This resulted in a late night by recent standards – it was well after 11pm by the time we got to bed. It had been a long day and choosing our wedding rings had made up for the transitory disappointments of Queenstown being too busy and Stewart Island being closed. We'd return at least to Queenstown but before then we were headed over the next few days, for what we both thought would be the main highlight of the trip, the wilderness area at New Zealand's south western corner known as Fiordland National Park.

Chapter Twelve
Sailing Westwards.

We'd decided that, according to the bird book the large bird we'd just seen by the roadside was a white heron. Apparently we were lucky to spot one as they are extremely rare. We're not quite Bill Oddie and Kate Humble but we had taken to looking out for different breeds of bird and ticking them off in the New Zealand bird book that we'd bought in Auckland. I'd been most impressed with the large buzzard – like Australian harriers though they did seem fairly common and the Weka's of Westland had amused us both. Jacqui, however, having given up looking for Pukeko's, which didn't seem so common in the south, was determined to see and tick off – of all things, the New Zealand Pigeon. It was similar to our own woodpigeon if a little larger but seemingly not as common, though the book said they inhabited most regions. Not that common as we hadn't seen one!

We set off again driving east away from Fiordland towards Dunedin – yes, I know we were going to Fiordland but we'd decided to do a bit of a loop to see more of the Southern Scenic Route and a bit of the Caitlins region. After

Fortrose we left the main road and followed the coastal route which was largely unsealed across open breezy grasslands to the lighthouse at Waipapa Point. The lighthouse was in a great spot but had a dark history. It was built in 1884 in response to the wreck of the Tararua in which 131 people sadly lost their lives. This was New Zealand's worst shipping disaster.

Continuing around coast our next stop was at Slope Point, the southernmost point of South Island which was reached by a walk across fields and had another signpost similar to the one at Bluff perched on the cliff top. The farmer tending his sheep would instantly know the answer if ever he was asked in the pub how far it was to London or Cape Town. A good spot again but I think Waipapa was a more impressive location. Our last stop on this road was the Petrified Forest at Curio Bay. It's from the Jurassic era around 180 million years ago and you can actually see the tree stumps and roots which are fossilised, unlike the ancient kauri wood we saw on North Island, protruding from the sand. We drove to Porpoise Bay before rejoining the main road and heading back towards Invercargill on our way to Fiordland.

Our trip up the coast had seemed further than we'd thought, mainly because of the unsealed roads but we were now keen to get to Manapouri in Fiordland. Crossing the main Invercargill road just outside town, it now seemed strangely familiar as though we'd spent more than simply a night there; we pressed on through Riverton and stopped for lunch by Colac Bay. We were at a pull in off a long straight road which ran along the shore and the van rocked slightly in the gusts as I ate my salami sandwich. The sky had turned grey and the windows showed there were drops of rain in the wind gusting in from the Southern Ocean. Outside it was deserted. Tussock grass bordered the road ruffling in the sharp gusts. The clumps of grass became fewer as the sandy ground became the empty beach before the eye was drawn to the white flecked grey of the rolling sea.

    The scene reminded me a lot of my childhood. When visiting our relatives in Barrow in Furness in Cumbria we'd drive down to the coast road just out of town. Invariably Mum and usually Gill, my sister, would opt to stay in the car leaving me and Dad to brave the elements and walk the beach until we too were driven back to the car by either rain or windblown sand. Yes, Colac Bay was an exposed and deserted spot but I liked it anyway. This coast was all like this especially as the weather began going downhill from then on. Further on we stopped briefly at a place called McCracken's Rest which was a viewing atop the cliffs overlooking the vast sweep of Tae Waewae Bay. Often, the rare Hector's Dolphins can be seen from here but they weren't around today, just a cow sheltering from the wind behind a hedge. The view across to Stewart Island was fantastic despite being half curtained by grey rain squalls, with the mountains of the Hump Ridge at the southern end of the Alps jutting out into the ocean at the western end of the bay.

On again inland, north and away from the coast, the rain set in as though it meant business as the road wound into the hills following the valley of the Waiau River through the small townships of Tuatapere and Clifden. I made a note to come back when the weather was better for a closer look at Clifden suspension bridge which was opened in 1899 to replace a rowing boat ferry.

Densely wooded mountains rose into swirling grey mist as we approached Manapouri and the light was fading behind the rain when we arrived at the lakeshore. We stopped and bought some supplies at the general store whose interior was right out of a 1950's movie before following the lake shore north 2 or 3 miles to reach the campsite called Manapouri Lake View which I'd found on the internet before we'd flown out here.

The Morris Minors here had never been filled with petrol for an onwards journey they were still here as part of a collection along with parts of aeroplanes and tractors. Kids would love this place. We did ourselves, so we immediately booked for 3 nights with a possible 4th in mind. Mrs. Nicholson, one of the owners, was also able to book the cruise on Doubtful Sound through local company Fiordland explorer Charters for the next day. We were really glad we did this as it turned out instead of using the big commercial operator.

The rain eased off before dark so we wandered around the site which also had log cabins and even houses all tastefully positioned in the middle of the dense rainforest, as was our campervan pitch. The toilets had cartoons and drawings on the walls and the whole place had a magical time warp atmosphere. Crossing the road brought us down to a little hidden beach on Lake Manapouri which had a fantastic view out across the calm water to wooded islands and misted peaks rising beyond distant shores. Only one bottle of wine that night as at 9am the next day we were to be picked up outside the site for our Doubtful Sound trip.

The following morning dawned chilly but bright and as the bus dropped us off at Manapouri's harbour it became clear we'd picked a good day. The rain was gone and a blue and white sky shone above the sparkling waters of the lake as Fiordland Explorer's motor cruiser headed out from Manapouri. There were only 9 of us on the tour which was led by a local guy called Mark who knew this area like the back of his hand. On the crossing of the lake he told us about the area's history of deer hunting whose rise and fall was pegged firmly to the price of Venison. The deer had been introduced as a money making scheme during times of high venison prices. When the prices fell, many deer were released into the wild as farming became uneconomic. When prices then went sky high, the deer's popularity was such that hunters would take to the hills with tales even of 'men of iron' leaping boldly from helicopters onto remote and inaccessible mountainsides in the effort to procure a supply of bambi burgers. Nowadays, the deer are still there but not so sought after, an occasional cull by DOC (Department of Conservation) keeping numbers under control.

The mountains rose above the lake on all sides, forest covered lower down and snow capped higher up, wild remote country in which to chase deer. Passing more wooded islands we neared the far side and disembarked at the jetty at the bottom of the West Arm of Lake Manapouri. This is a fantastic spot at the bottom of the Wilmot Pass which leads over to Deep Cove on Doubtful Sound. The forests descend to the sheltered lake shore, the mountains rise serenely above and the only sound is that of forest birds and the lapping of the water against the jetty. It's hard to believe then that this is the site of one the country's largest electric power stations.

The Manapouri underground power station is a feat of engineering. Housed in great cavernous halls deep beneath the mountains the hydro electric plant shows no outward signs from above other than the line of pylons and the entrance tunnel. No sound of machinery is heard above ground and no greenhouse gases or other pollution is emitted to the environment. Oh and did I forget to mention – the energy's free – it falls from the sky. The tour of the station before we continued to Doubtful Sound was quite fascinating; you take a bus down through the tunnel to the site of the plant. There's no heat or smoke as the electricity is generated from water power, exploiting the height difference between Lake Manapouri at 177m and the outlet near Deep Cove at sea level. The trip is rather like the "Electric Mountain" at Llanberis in North Wales but on a much larger scale. For me, who gets particularly annoyed at wanton destruction of natural environments and irresponsible pollution, I do think that Manapouri is an example of how things should be done. If we do really need the amount of energy we use then a greater percentage should come from sites like this. They had in fact just finished a project to widen the drainage shafts' increasing the generation capacity of the plant which I believe is now around 850 Mw..

When we returned back to the daylight, we boarded our bus for the short journey over Wilmot Pass to Doubtful Sound. Mark tied up the motor launch and turned bus driver for this leg of the trip – a man of many talents! The narrow road winds up through the trees from West Arm climbing gradually to something like 670m at the Wilmot Pass Saddle. Here the weather changed again, the cool crisp morning became cold and damp as the cloud pressed in to the bus windows at the summit. We were of course heading back to the west coast again and the vegetation became much lusher on the other side as we negotiated a steep tortuous descent.

We came down below the mist with Doubtful Sound spread out below us set in a deep green forest scape of steep hillsides. After passing a few points on the road where the more nervous passengers opted to close their eyes and hope that Mark was as good with a bus as with a boat, we finally levelled out and wound around the head of the fiord to Deep Cove which was a small harbour set in the rainforest in the awesome silence of Doubtful Sound. With the mist hanging over the still waters and the tree covered mountainsides draped with waterfalls, it was hard to imagine a finer spot. However, there lurked here a menace from which grown men will run and which strikes terror into the hearts of even the hardiest of wilderness campers. They are a scourge to rival the "scurrilous wee beasties" that plague the Scottish Islands and sea lochs.

Milford Sound to the north has a headland named Sandfly Point and for a very good reason. The game is given away by the name but we were fore-armed. The fearsome sandfly has a chink in its armour. It has a maximum cruising speed of – yes – 5 to 6km per hour or in laymen's terms a fairly quick walk. I tested this whilst waiting to board our boat at the harbour and yes, it worked. Standing still invited attack but even a steady walk up and down the harbour front completely prevented me from being bitten. OK, it's not much use if you're camping but useful to know!

Mark was back sailing again as our second boat of the morning headed out into the sound. We could stay inside and listen to his commentary or go up top for a better view. The damp weather here was possibly milder than at Manapouri but it wasn't that warm so everyone kind of alternated. Sailing westwards the scenery of the sound was some of the best I'd seen, waterfalls coming down out of the clouds and the ever present trees clinging to impossibly steep slopes. The rocks of the walls were covered with moss layers adding to the greenery and the mist clinging to the mountains just made the whole place more atmospheric. In odd places the rock walls were bare of trees. This was caused by so called tree avalanches. There's no real soil layer on the steep slopes so the trees anchor into a layer of moss coating the rocks. Where this breaks away a whole section will come down.

After some time we sailed past the southern inlet of crooked arm, a branch of the main fiord and Mark switched off the engine so we could sit up top and experience the silence of the place, Carrying on westwards towards the open sea which was still along way off and invisible, its over 20 miles from Deep Cove to the Tasman Sea, the enclosing walls gave us the feeling more of being on a lake than the sea. That was, until the Dolphins arrived. Ten or twelve of them appeared and swam alongside us as they had at the Bay of Islands. They were bottlenose dolphins as well, the same type. Somehow, no-one fancied taking a dip with them this time, these southern waters were not as inviting as around sub-tropical Bay of Islands!

This trip often sails out around a large island bird sanctuary called Secretary Island but today, despite the calm here, there were rough conditions in the open sea beyond so we crossed to the northern side of the sound just east of the island in a place called Blanket Bay. Here we stopped for lunch once the dolphins had gone their separate way. We all sat up top and drank a brew Mark had done below deck, and had lunch. With the engines off once more we were able to simply enjoy the silence and appreciate our position. A tiny boat in the middle of a vastness of nature, not a sign of human habitation could be seen.

Looking at the shoreline here I thought it would be good to find a patch of level ground and camp out until I remembered the sandflies – there were none out here in the middle of the Sound! The voyage back to Deep Cove was interrupted when someone spotted a couple of penguins on the shore. We went closer and the engine was turned off so as not to disturb them too much. They were Fiordland Crested Penguins native to this area and are much smaller than the kings or emperors that we're used to seeing on nature programmes. The penguins were quite funny, when they perceived a threat, i.e. us; they turned their back on us to pretend we weren't there. They were fairly well camouflaged until, until turning round to see if we'd really gone they revealed a large yellow mark on the side of their heads which could be seen a mile away!

Mark showed us one of the so called 'temporary' waterfalls which were supposed to dry up at intervals. A massive flow of water crashed down from the heights into the fiord and he said that despite visiting the area for over 20 years hunting and fishing he'd never known it to dry up!

Too soon we were back at Deep Cove for the return over Wilmot Pass and he reassured the passengers who had closed their eyes last time that he'd never gone over the edge in the bus. With the sunset behind us we made the return crossing of Lake Manapouri. The cloud and mist had gone on this side and it had been a fine day if a little chilly. Back into Manapouri and there was frost in the air as we headed off to a restaurant in nearby Te Anau for an evening meal, neither of us feeling like cooking after our long day.

Was this the best day trip in the world? Well, there are plenty I've not done so I can't really answer that one but it's got to be up there with them. Besides, the next day was Milford Sound which also promised great things.

Chapter Thirteen
Milford Deep

The Milford road is one of the world's great scenic highways. It journeys from Te Anau for 72 miles to Milford Sound on the west coast, famous for that view of Mitre Peak rising sheer above the water, which appears on so many calendars and in just about every book or tourist brochure about New Zealand, including this one I might add!

It was both a good and bad thing to drive the road in the winter months. We wouldn't get the hoards of tourists who flock to Milford Sound in the summer but there were downsides. The road reaches an altitude of 945 metres, over 3000 feet, and is frequently affected by snow and ice at this time of year. Even more of a hazard is the snow that falls down off the mountains rising as high again above the road. In fact avalanches are the main reason for closure and there's a no stopping rule on parts of the road to reduce the time spent in the danger zone. OK, snow or traffic jams? Er - let me think about that – yeah give me snow every time!

We had in fact learned that the road had just re-opened yesterday after a huge avalanche had come down so the danger was no idle threat either, but we were also told that we wouldn't need snow chains for the van. In certain weather it's mandatory to carry them.

Surprisingly enough, we were in the photo shop in Te Anau, maybe about 10 miles north of our campsite, early that morning. Actually it wasn't really a photo shop but a chemist which kind of did the photo shop thing, putting photos on disc and developing films. We'd driven down here in patchy freezing fog but the weather forecast was good for the day which is just as well as Milford is among the wettest places in the world, with 8000mm of rain annually which makes even the Lake District and North Wales seem like the Sahara.

So to the accompaniment of an audio CD commentary we'd bought from the garage to give the "authentic coach trip" feel, we began our journey to Milford. The CD turned out to be quite useful once we'd both stopped laughing at the cheesy voice on the commentary, as it did point out, in plenty of time, the best places to stop on the route. We were able to time our stops to avoid the 2 or 3 coach parties on the road at the same time. The journey led firstly through the tussock country north along the eastern shore of Lake Te Anau before climbing right away from the lake at Te Anau downs and entering a long valley. Here the sun broke through and the mist cleared revealing white frosted grasslands and trees beneath a cloudless blue sky of exceptional clarity. The snow covered mountains ahead rose gradually nearer dazzling white against the deep blue.

We stopped for a while at Mirror Lakes which lived up to their name today, there wasn't a breath of wind, and then stopped again at Lake Gunn. Our last stop before the 'no stopping' zone was near a place called The Divide where the famous Routeburn Track heads off to near Glenorchy on the far side of the mountains to the east. It's a 3 day hike and one I'd love to do but not at this time of year, it's definitely a summer season hike. We thought about maybe walking up to Key Summit, the first section but we wouldn't have time today.

Next, came a fantastic view down the Hollyford valley which looked a stunning spot, before we headed westwards and the road began to wind as it made its ascent of the mountains. The snowy peaks towered overhead now on both sides as the road climbed a gorge like valley. The trees became patchy and the surroundings opened out into an alpine landscape. The tracks of past avalanches were clearly seen and at one point the trees had been flattened by an avalanche. I'd seen this destruction once before in Norway and it definitely made you want to get through the avalanche zone as quickly as possible!

We entered a huge cirque in the mountain, the snow now reaching down to the road and accentuating the dazzling brightness of the sun in the clear blue sky overhead. I needed my sunglasses just to see enough to drive. We passed huge piles of snow and ice, the debris from the last avalanche to close the road the week before, and reached the point where the road disappeared into the sheer rock wall barring the way. The Homer tunnel is unlit, or was at the time, and the contrast from the dazzling sunlight and snow to the tunnel's blackness was such that I had to stop the van to let my eyes adjust. Even with glasses off and lights on, I couldn't see a thing!

We presently emerged back into bright sunlight though there was less snow on this side. The road descended quickly in a wide sweep below grey cliffs, down which cascaded an impressive waterfall turned partly to huge icicles hanging from the cliff. Our descent continued steeply and soon we were back in the lush greenery of Fiordland's forests. Pulling in at a nearly empty car park just short of Milford Sound we had our first meeting with the kea. The kea is a breed of parrot native to New Zealand; in fact it's the only parrot which lives in alpine areas. The birds have a reputation for cheekiness. This is born partly out of a liking, similar to that of safari park monkeys, for any detachable parts from cars such as windscreen wiper rubbers, window seals etc and in fact anything that the birds consider vaguely edible or simply worth investigating.

A tour guide was attempting to entice one bird out that had taken up residence under their minibus while the other bird was being fed on banana and peanuts that were intended as a bribe for its mate under the van. The bird sitting under the van showed no sign of coming out and the other one was quite happy to continue being fed. In fact he looked as though they'd planned it between them. "Right I'm hungry, your turn under the car!"

Carrying on, we drove another ten minutes or so before turning a corner and having one of those moments similar to when you first see the Matterhorn or the Eiffel Tower, you've never been before but the scene looks so familiar because you've seen it on hundreds of postcards. Through the trees, Milford Sound had appeared in front of us. The blue water was almost mirror calm and there stood Mitre Peak, its top half plastered with snow, rising 5300 feet into the sky, on the far shore.

Our first priority, after Jacqui getting that classic photo, was to get on a boat trip. We booked onto the Real Journey's Milford sound cruise which would give us a tour of the fiord and time to call at the underwater observatory, Milford Deep on the way back. As the boat left port that bit of knowledge about the sandflies came in useful again. We were able to get a good spot on the deck at the front which was almost empty as the hordes below deck presumed they would be eaten alive if they came up. Unfortunately they cottoned on in the end and the peace was shattered. Milford was if anything more dramatic than Doubtful. It was necessary to crane one's neck right back to see where some of the cliffs ended and where the waterfalls came down from. Doubtful had the edge on atmosphere though. This wasn't helped when not only was the top deck invaded by the hordes from below braving the cold and the lack of sandflies, that wasn't a problem as it was a big boat; there was enough room for all, but a loudspeaker commentary started up with the volume of Bon Jovi playing Madison Square Gardens, sadly though without the tunefulness.

Once the commentator had pointed out to anyone within about 10 miles of us what we were sailing past, the commentary was repeated in Japanese, then Korean and several other languages until we came to the next point of interest and the whole thing started again. Any wildlife was certain to be deaf or well away with that racket going on. I know some people like to have a commentary but it doesn't need to be at 120 decibels. On Doubtful Sound we'd been given the choice, look through the window from the warmth of the cabin and listen to the tour guide or brave the elements and enjoy the peace and grandeur of nature at its best.

Despite the noise, the trip still ranked as a highlight. There we were in one of the wettest places on Earth looking up at surrounding mountains outlined against a clear blue sky and lit by a bright winter sun. It wasn't until you went outside you realised it wasn't midsummer. The boat headed along the fiord past Mitre Peak and around a headland to the open sea before turning around. This was the point that Captain Cook who discovered New Zealand and mapped most of its features famously sailed past so missing Milford Sound completely. The entrance was hard to spot from the sea if you didn't know it was there though! The inlet is much shorter than Doubtful Sound but the most impressive thing was that in places Milford is only 600 metres across, yet the enclosing walls rise over 1500 metres above the water, so its somewhat like sailing in the bottom of a trench.

On the return journey, just before we reached port the boat stopped to drop a number of us off at Milford Deep, the underwater observatory. It's quite fascinating as you go down 10.4 metres or about 35 feet below the waves down a spiral staircase to look out at the undersea world through thick glass windows. It's like being in an aquarium but it's just the open sea outside and you can see whatever swims up to the side of the sound. I wonder what people's reactions would have been had a big shark made an appearance! Josh, my son, would love this place. Whenever he's come on holiday with us he was guaranteed to find an aquarium which we'd all have to march round. It is several times now we've been to the Blue Planet near my parent's home to walk through the glass tunnel in the shark pool.

Milford Deep's definitely a must see if you're coming here, but I think the best way to see the Sound would be by Kayak if you're experienced enough. They do hire them out here, though it would be cold today, that's if I could get past my fear of capsizing!

Back to the van and off again after a brew. The journey back seemed longer but we were both tired by now. The cold returned with the evening and we were glad to be back at the site and have the heating on. It had been another busy but exciting day and almost as good was relaxing at the end with some wine. There was no rush to get up tomorrow as we'd planned to see the Te Anau glow worm caves but not until the afternoon!

The following morning proved highly productive if the aim was indeed to impersonate a cat. We both did next to nothing after breakfast other than laze around in the sun which streamed through the van windows. I normally like to be out doing something so it shows we probably needed the rest. I managed to finish one of my many books abut Mount Everest but that was about all!

Heading to the glow worm caves after an early lunch saw us park up in Te Anau and board the launch for the quite rough crossing of Lake Te Anau. The weather was still fine but a strong wind gusted along the lake forming some fairly hefty waves. Needless to say we all remained inside the cabin for the crossing to the caves as every so often a wave would actually break over the top of our boat.

Did I mention before that apart from capsizing in a canoe, one thing that's guaranteed to strike terror into my heart is the idea of potholing? I remember at a place I used to work there was this guy from Stoke who used to work as a miner in the Stoke coalfield. When they'd closed the pit and he'd had a career change he'd taken up the sport as a weekend activity. I thought he'd have had enough of holes in the ground but no – he loved it. Every time he suggested I come along though I'd always had an excuse not to. It was just this idea of squeezing through narrow passages which always seem to be half full of water in the films about caving I've seen.

These were my thoughts as we prepared to go into the Te Anau glow worm caves. There are two kinds of cave – those with nice wide passages that you can walk upright in and those that I don't go in! Thankfully this was the first kind. Once we'd gone through the entrance which was a little bit narrow and was where the river emerged from inside the mountain, I really enjoyed the experience. It was lit inside so we didn't need head torches or anything and we followed a wide passage to a series of steps built up a tunnel with the river below. The river in fact has eroded this whole cave system which goes for miles through the limestone beneath these mountains.

We didn't have to walk that far though as we came to a flooded cavern which the river drained from. Now we took to rafts and were pulled along a cable by our guide. Entering an unlit section as your eyes became adjusted to the blackness, thousands of points of light became visible overhead. It was like gazing up at the night sky and a totally surreal experience considering we were in a cave and drifting on an underground lake. Once I'd got the idea we were going to sink out of my head I found it a most relaxing experience.

The glow worms are actually insects larvae and the phosphorescent light is to attract food in the form of moths or other insects but the scene is of a myriad stars gathered in unfamiliar constellations and is really quite mystical. The Maori name of Te Ana–au is translated to mean "the cave with the current of swirling water" so it would seem that the locals knew of these caves long before they were rediscovered by Lawson Burrows in 1948.

That evening saw us preparing, somewhat sadly, to travel again the next day. Neither of us wanted to leave Fiordland as we both loved the place but we needed to go if we wanted to see Queenstown and Mount Cook before we had to return to England.

Chapter Fourteen
Pigeon Day!

The 20th August saw us heading back down through Manapouri and following the main highway out of town to the south, the way we'd come up from Invercargill. It was my mum's birthday today so I'd need to find a phone later and ring her. Working it out was still yesterday in England if that makes any sense, so I'd need to ring tonight which should be morning back home.

Our first destination of the day was Lake Hauroko. This is New Zealand's deepest lake and is in a fabulously remote setting 20 miles off the main highway. The lake is reached by turning off in a westerly direction just after Clifden and along the Hauroko Road; another gravel road through it wasn't particularly rough or difficult to drive on. The road passed a few very isolated farms and we saw just one other car in the 20 mile trip. It was another vast landscape the wide valley leading the eye towards the distant mountains which we headed slowly towards. Once the last farm was passed there was no sign of human habitation at all other than the road itself which presently entered an area of native bush for the last few miles to the lake.

The Lake Hauroko campground is basically a clearing at the end of this dirt track and looked like a good place to camp. Not this time though as we had further to go that day. We had a short walk along the deserted shore line and out along a small jetty which gave good views of the lake and the mountains surrounding us on three sides. This must have been where the boat sailed you to the start (or finish) of the Dusky track at the far end of the lake. This is one of the country's toughest and most remote hiking trails and links Lake Hauroko with Supper Cove on the inaccessible Dusky Sound and finally Lake Manapouri close to where we'd seen the underground power station. Both ends of the Dusky Track are therefore only accessible by boat.

There were a few sandflies about here so after a walk we decided to go back inside the van for an early lunch rather than sit out on the beach. The insects may be easy to avoid by waking but sit still and you'll know they are there all right! Just as we re-entered the clearing where we'd parked we both heard a noise in the trees above that made us stop in our tracks. I instantly recognised the sound, as at my parents' house we always had a pair of wood pigeons living in the trees behind. The bird crashed through some leaves before winging its way in leisurely fashion under the branches before being lost to sight in the surrounding woods.

The New Zealand woodpigeon is larger and had more colour in its feathers than the dirty grey variety that inhabits places like Trafalgar square. Jacqui was as chuffed as a train at finally spotting one and I was almost as chuffed at the fact that she'd seen one! Rain was once again in the air as we finished the 20 miles in the other direction and turned back onto the main road. It was odd driving on tarmac after 40 miles on gravel. Before continuing though I pulled in at a lay-by so we could see the Clifden suspension bridge. It's a most impressive wooden structure spanning the Waiau River and is well worth stopping to have a closer look at.

Back on the road again and this time heading through farming communities with names like Birchwoods and Nightcaps as well as a few one horse towns. The absence of petrol stations became more noticeable the further we went and the lower the gauge got. Soon the garage in Winton became our goal rather than simply Winton. With the petrol gauge needle firmly into the red bit, I turned right on the now familiar highway 6 and drove at 30mph the last two miles into Winton where we reached the garage in the nick of time!

It was as we headed back up that stretch of road in the direction of Queenstown that there was a most curious sighting by the roadside. We'd just left Winton and Jacqui who was driving had slowed down behind a tractor in front. As the tractor turned off, just past the turning on the grass verge was what looked at first like Big Bird from Sesame Street. As we drove past, the mysterious creature revealed itself to be an Ostrich trotting purposefully in the direction of Winton.

"Did I just see what I thought I just saw or am I seeing things?" I asked Jacqui and she replied that she'd just seen it as well. I wasn't seeing things.

"I don't think", she added "that I'll see any of those in the New Zealand bird book!"

I can only assume that the bird had escaped from an ostrich farm somewhere about here and was no doubt enjoying its new found freedom in a land renowned for a variety of flightless birds and a complete lack of lions or other threats.

After the Ostrich incident, the journey was uneventful and we soon found ourselves back in the Scottish landscape leading back along Lake Wakatipu. Passing the Frankton campsite we turned left and came to Queenstown. This time we headed straight through town and on along the shores of Lake Wakatipu as the sun sunk lower in the sky over the mountains in front. The road, still following the lake on our left, did a sharp right and headed more to the north finally reaching the end of Wakatipu at the small settlement of Glenorchy.

I mentioned to Jacqui that I'd camped at Glenorchy, the one in Scotland, years before and this was a similar spot, a broad remote valley surrounded by mountains. Another place in fact of stunning scenery! The small shop here was pretty much the centre of town and it was here we booked on to the campsite, bought some wine and food and picked up some leaflets on walks in the area. If you wanted to sail by steamship to Queenstown or ride on the river Dart jet boats you could arrange that here too.

We got the van set up before venturing out into the cold darkness to the phone outside the site shop. I wished my mum a happy birthday from 12000 miles away. It was strange being so far away from home with my mum and dad preparing to go and drink tea in the garden on a summer morning while it was a cold winters evening at this end of the line. Back in the van I cooked chilli and rice, suitable food for the weather I thought. We had begun to think of the van's gas bottle as being magic as it was still going strong after all this time and once again it didn't fail us. After our meal it was a case of planning our next few days of the trip and drinking wine. We decided to do a walk up here near Glenorchy before heading back to Queenstown and staying on one of the town centre campsites. This would avoid having to drive in and out of town too much. We could just leave the van set up then.

Sunday morning was quiet in Glenorchy but then probably every morning is quiet here. We were the only vehicle on the road as we headed up valley on what soon became dirt roads. We crossed a bridge over the River Dart to the west bank and continued to head north up the valley towards the massive snowy bulk of Mount Earnslaw.

This valley was another location in Lord of the Rings, Isengard, though there was no sign of Saruman's stone tower of Orthanc! We'd decided to do the walk to Sylvan Lake which began at a small car park occupied by single car by the side of the gravel road. The walk is a couple of hours so was about right for that morning and gave us a chance to experience the landscape of this region. The way led through the forest which here was mainly beech trees. Different to the denser native bush of the damper west coast, there's little undergrowth and even in the denser patches plenty of light reaches the forest floor. This means that you walk in a pale green twilight rather than the semi darkness of the rainforest.

After crossing a rope bridge over the fast flowing Routeburn River the way continued through the beech trees which were apparently another "Rings" location. The area had been used as the setting for Lochlorien, home of the elves of the wood. Unfortunately, Cate Blanchett wasn't to be seen anywhere.

Lake Sylvan is one of those places I'm always reluctant to leave. You emerge from the pale green light and almost musical rustling of the beech trees to sunlight and the gentle lapping of water on a small stony beach surrounded by the woods. We had lunch here to the sound of trees, water and the birds. We even seemed sheltered from the cold breeze which gusted down the valley moving the tree tops above us. Walking back to the van we had an encounter with a pair of robins. The New Zealand robin is similar in shape to our familiar red breast if slightly smaller but is grey coloured without the red. They came very close, seemingly curious as to whom these visitors were and when Jacqui photographed them they were almost sat on our boots they were so close. Like the fantails which are known for following people along the trails here, it's the insects we disturb that attracts them rather than a curiosity to meet us. Nice idea though!

Back at the van I checked the map for our way back to Queenstown and realised that the Routeburn Track started near here. It takes roughly three days and goes from this valley over the mountains to the Hollyford Valley where we'd stopped on our way to Milford. That was definitely a priority for our next trip to New Zealand.

The way back was easy, just retracing our route up here back to the tarmac highway at Glenorchy and along Lake Wakatipu. The view ahead revealed a range of mountains known as the Remarkables, topped by Double Cone, another summer objective, rising above Queenstown.

Jacqui drove into town and I managed to navigate without difficulty to the Queenstown Top 10 holiday park, called Creeksyde. It was easier not having to find parking and it didn't seem as busy anyway. The site was down a side road and though the busiest site we'd been on since Wellington, was in a really good spot. You could walk into town yet we were camped in the trees with a small stream just beside us. The facilities here were some of the best we'd seen as well and would enable us to get everything thoroughly clean and dry.

Before tea we had a walk to the nearby Kiwi Bird life Park which was an hour well spent. Most of the country's native birds including Kiwi's can be seen either outdoors or inside a curious large tube-like structure which you walk through. An original design I thought. They also had a model of a traditional Maori village from pre-European days which was the first sign of old Maori culture we'd seen since leaving North Island.

As we left Jacqui took a really good photo of the sun setting on the Remarkables opposite while back at the van we decided that, because we could, we'd go out for tea. We found a pizza place in town via a bar and ended up back in the bar after tea. In this way we managed not only to eat out but for the first time since Auckland have a proper night out!

Chapter Fifteen
Return to Queenstown

The following day was one of catching up with the world after our relative isolation of the previous week or so. The busy streets and shops served only to remind me why we'd gone off in the van in the first place! Seriously though it was a welcome change, for a day or two at any rate! Queenstown's main street is like the main street of any tourist centre in the mountains. It could be Fort William, Keswick. Breckenridge or Chamonix apart from one thing, in addition to the usual streets of outdoor gear and ski hire shops, every other shop front seemed to be advertising some bizarre way of trying to kill yourself – or that's what it looked like! There were banners beckoning the tourist to dive headlong out of aircraft, hang upside down over a river on the end of a big rubber band, fly a plane on a wire up a narrow gorge, you name it, it was there along with photos of the participants in varying states of terror.

Personally I quite fancied the idea of jumping from a high mountain with a parachute or hurtling along a narrow river in a speedboat, inches from the rocks. Jacqui also liked the idea of the jet boat ride and this being the world famous

Shotover Jet we had to have a go. We booked a trip for that afternoon and proceeded to wander aimlessly around the shops in the meantime. The tandem parapente jump I'd possibly do the next day or when the wind died down a bit. If I was going to do it I wanted to do it form the highest jump point available which was Coronet Peak at nearly 6000 feet.

 I decided to buy my son Josh a New Zealand All Blacks rugby shirt so we headed for a clothing store. Here I saw a particularly amusing t-shirt which read in big bold letters,

"I support two teams – New Zealand and whoever's playing Australia"

This was the constant rivalry and competition between the Kiwis and the Aussies. I remembered a guy on a website while I was researching this trip and he'd said, "New Zealand has four islands; North Island, South Island, Stewart Island and the West Island, which some people call Australia!" Just no respect for "The Land of Warney"! I thought about copying the t-shirt idea and having one made back home declaring support for anyone who was playing Manchester United. I'm not that big on football myself but I thought of when I worked at an office in Wilmslow. We'd a German girl working there at the time and on the day Man United were to play a German side, Leverkusen; I think it was, she was unable to understand why all these English guys were supporting the German side.

 After fish and chips for lunch we boarded the bus to take us to the Shotover Jet. The Shotover River at this point flows through a narrow rocky gorge in a series of rapids and is a most impressive sight. It is also this section of river that you negotiate at, what must be, over 50 mph! I'd been on Zodiac type fast boats before but out at sea. The big red jet boat, with immense power and manoeuvrability, did two runs of the narrowest and rockiest section of the gorge at great speed and so close to the walls that they were almost a blur. It was a totally awesome experience and we were both buzzing for at least an hour after getting off. Thrill therapy is what they call this ride and yeah, that describes it pretty well! In one of the pauses in the adrenaline rush, our driver had told us about one of my childhood heroes, New Zealander Ed Hillary going most of the way up the Ganges in one of these things. Not a bad job to have, hey!

We were up fairly early the next morning as we'd decided to have a go at Ben Lomond, the mountain that rose above Queenstown. The ascent began with a ride on the Skyline Gondola. The small four seat cabin rises from 340 metres at Queenstown steeply up to 790 metres at the Skyline Restaurant which was actually visible almost directly above our campsite. The view from here was amazing. Queenstown spread out below and the blue grey expanse of Lake Wakatipu. On the far side of the valley over the hill known as Deer Park Heights rose the Remarkables range, their pointed summits shrouded in cloud.

Setting out up the path, we passed the summer luge and I planned to have a go on the way back if we had the time. The wide path led up into the woods beyond the luge before turning a corner to the right and emerging from the trees after a short drop. From here, snow covered Ben Lomond was visible or rather its lower part was, the cloud having come in higher up.

The path headed on up the grass hillside passing through a small copse-like wood oddly positioned halfway up the slope. The weather became more marginal with spots of rain gusting down from a grey ceiling. We decided to go to the col ahead, the Ben Lomond Saddle and call it a day unless things improved. We began walking through patches of melting snow in the heather before ascending a long bumpy ridge with steep slopes falling away on either side. The snow became deeper and the view behind over Lake Wakatipu more spectacular the higher we got until we finally emerged in showers of sleet at the col.

This was at 4300 feet or about 1300 metres and with the conditions we decided to go no further. There was another couple there who had decided the same so the 4 of us sat and ate our lunches on a bench overlooking the far side of the ridge into a remote looking valley. The ridge up to Ben Lomond looked easy enough but in the deep snow and with the weather going downhill fast we set off back down pausing to watch the steamship TSS Earnslaw make its way slowly up the lake below.

Our decision to come down was vindicated when we were caught up by an American guy coming down the mountain behind us. He said that he'd gone up to within 50 yards of the summit and could go no further because of waist deep snow. We'd done the right thing, the rain set in properly just as we approached the Gondola station so I even opted to miss the luge ride.

Back at the site we had a lazy evening just planning the trip to Mount Cook and a possible Parapente jump the next day weather permitting.

The weather didn't permit, the cloud was right down almost to the valley so there'd be no parapenting that day, not from anywhere least of all from Coronet Peak. We packed up and headed first of all for Arrowtown stopping off at the Hackett Bungy on the way. A couple of victims hurled themselves into space while we watched from the observation area and Jacqui categorically banned me from having a go myself. I was all too eager to accept the ban and didn't argue my corner at all, feeling certain guilt that I should have been up there having a go myself. The jump reservation desk beckoned mockingly to me as we walked past and an annoying little song became stuck in my head;
"Chick, chick, chick, chick, chicken,
Lay a little egg for me.
Chick, chick, chick, chick, chicken,
I want one for my tea......"
As we drove into Arrowtown it was still there;
"And now it's half past three
So chick, chick, chick, chick, chicken.... "

Arrowtown reminds one of a theme park version of Hokitika. The town itself is nice enough and pleasant to walk round but the shops seemed expensive and full of tourists and the streets crowded. Despite the contrived appearance, Arrowtown is far from contrived. It was built by miners in 1862 when gold was discovered in the nearby Arrow River. It's a place of well maintained but original wooden buildings along a wide unpaved street similar to the towns of the old Wild West.

The rain had stopped but the mist hung around the lower slopes of the hills as we headed down the valley out of the Queenstown area. Our way led over the high Crown Range Pass, the road climbing hairpin bends up into the mist before a long viewless ascent to the top. On the far side of the pass we emerged from the mist and descended into a wild and sparsely populated land of sweeping ridges and open tussock hills. Passing the Cadrona Ski area the road led on to Wanaka at the southern end of the lake of the same name.

Lake Wanaka once again sparkled blue in a sun that shown with little warmth, a cold wind fuelling the waves on its vast surface. The snowy summits of the Mount Aspiring region dazzled beyond the far shore as the cloud broke overhead and raced white across the blue. We walked on the lake front before enjoying a coffee in the van sheltered from the wind.

From Wanaka we continued our journey to a lunch stop at a roadside café in Tarras in the lower part of the Lindis Valley. Here the land was almost treeless, a region of wide tussock grasslands, windswept and sparsely populated. Despite its remoteness the café was quite busy for lunch. The food was excellent in fact so people probably came here from elsewhere around.

The weather had now changed totally, though it was still chilly, the sun shone from a clear blue sky and it was hard to believe the wind and rain we'd left behind. The road snaked across another vast landscape; in places looking quite arid for this was the rain shadow of the Southern Alps. The mountains ahead were rounded rather than jagged but their snow cover indicated they were of great height as the road climbed steadily to the Lindis Pass.

Our next stop was the curiously named Twizel in the plains on the far side of the pass. It was a very tidy looking place, almost too clean. There was no litter or cars in the street, not even any people. The place seemed deserted, until we went into the supermarket for some food. It seemed the whole population were in there, most of them just stood in the aisles chatting to each other. It felt almost like being in a Stephen King movie as though something strange was just about to happen, or maybe this was what they did in Twizel on Wednesdays. Back into the deserted streets and another Stephen King moment when we had trouble finding the road out of town. The signs led us in a big circle before we found the way back to the highway. We thought that the people in the supermarket had just popped in to buy a few groceries on the way somewhere and had been prevented from leaving! More like the Twilight Zone than Stephen King really!

When we finally found our way back to the main road we followed it across the wide grassy plains, for this was sheep country, towards a distant line of high jagged peaks seeming to rise straight up from the grasslands. It reminded me of the view across the open plains from Denver, Colorado towards the line of the Rockies. As we approached nearer, the highest of the peaks took on a familiar appearance and I recognized it as Mount Cook from the photos I'd seen.

The waters of Lake Pukaki were to our right and presently we pulled in at a small car park called "Peter's Lookout". I commented to Jacqui that if I was indeed going to own a 'lookout' then this one would do though she did say I might have some competition from her Dad, who's also called Pete and loves the mountains as much as I do!

The sun was setting behind the snow of the Southern Alps as we reached our campsite. We'd opted for the Glen Tanner site which was just past the end of the lake near a wide braided river bed. The highest peaks in New Zealand rose at the end of the valley dominated by Mount Cook or Aoraki to give it its Maori name. More high summits towered on both sides of the valley and back the way we'd come was a hint of the distant places we'd left behind.

There was a DOC site at Mount Cook village nearer to the peak but it didn't have electric hook-ups. We didn't want to risk being without heating in what would be our coldest night since leaving Whakapapa. Our trusty everlasting gas bottle hadn't let us down so far but it couldn't really last for ever. It was hard to believe that just over the mountains were Fox and Franz Josef glaciers where we'd camped. The open grass and scrubland here couldn't have been more different. We had a short troll round the site and Jacqui photographed the sunset on Mount Cook before we retired to the warmth of the van for the evening.

Chapter Sixteen
The 1255 Steps

Jacqui was up at dawn photographing the sunrise on Mount Cook at the end of the valley. I was quite content to look through the window while I completed the slow process of waking up, staying warm in the process. The day promised good things though, as the snowfields above the valley glowed first rose pink then orange before building into a white glare against a deep blue sky as the sun gained strength, the valley still in twilight. Presently though the sun reached us too and began to melt the frost from the grass outside.

Over our toast and boiled eggs we planned our last full day in the van. Tomorrow we handed our home back to the Apollo office at Christchurch airport and would fly back to Auckland. Trying not to dwell too much on having to go home, we decided on driving up to Mount Cook Village, having a look round and going for a walk probably up to Red Tarns which was a marked path up from the village.

It was a morning of wall to wall sunshine as we drove the few miles to the end of the valley. The bare mountainsides rose almost sheer from the flat alluvial plain that formed the valley floor. There were trees clinging to some of the slopes and patchy scrubland but it lacked the forests of the European Alps or the Rockies. Above the small cluster of buildings making up the village, hung the huge glaciers shining blue white in the sun and above them the jagged rock and ice of the highest peaks of the Southern Alps.

We parked up near the visitor centre, we'd look around there when we got down, and set off along the trail past the public shelter towards Red Tarns. Considering how good the weather was there wasn't a soul around as we followed the path down a shady slope to the Black Birch Stream which descended from the mountains in a steep sided gorge. Once across the footbridge the path climbed steeply up the far side. The Department of Conservation (DOC) had constructed stone steps here from the rocks to facilitate progress and as we turned the corner to the right it became apparent that the steps continued well past the initial steep section. The way led up through trees and it soon became hot. There was hardly a breath of wind and the slope we climbed was something of a sun trap. Still the steps led upwards, now above the trees up a bare hillside the gorge of the Black Birch far below on the right and the towering white ramparts of Mount Cook above the Hooker Glacier across the valley with Mount Sefton nearer at hand to their left.

My thoughts tended to keep returning to subjects such as Stone Age rockers Led Zeppelin's song "Stairway to Heaven" and what it would be like if the lifts broke down when you lived on 102nd floor of the Empire State Building.

We resolved to count these steps on the way down as they way surpassed our recent experiences of the Eiffel Tower and Notre Dame in Paris. At long last the stone stairway levelled out and became wooden boards as we reached Red Tarns. Unlike their namesake "Red Tarn" on Helvellyn, in the English Lakes, the tarns were really pools, reddish from the pond weed and set in a mossy hollow of the mountainside. The view across the valley gave away the true scale of the mountains at its head with the village 1300 feet below at the end of the thin strip of road we'd driven up earlier. The water of the tarns themselves was clear as crystal and gave a perfect reflection of the mountains opposite, while all around was the silence and immense grandeur of nature,

We sat for a while by the pools absorbing this scene before making the knee-jarring descent back to the van. We did remember to count the stone steps on the way back revealing what they don't tell you in the walks leaflets, that the Red Tarns Track could equally be named "The 1255 steps"! Returning over the bridge it was now quite a warm morning and a couple of paradise ducks had gathered expectantly close to the car park, clearly expecting more tourists. We saw only one other person on the way back through the village though. We had a quick look around the visitor centre where I bought "View From the Summit" Edmund Hillary's autobiography before we headed back down the valley past the campsite at Glentanner and along the shores of Lake Pukaki, the water a bright blue green in the sunlight from particles in the glacial streams.

At the end of the lake we turned back onto highway 8 before Twizel and journeyed in the general direction of Christchurch. The country here was predominantly grassland with lines of green hills leading the eye to the left where the distant white peaks of the Alps shone in the sun. Lunch was at a café by the shore of Lake Tekapu which looked as though it was a popular spot in summer but today it was only us in the large dining area enjoying the view of the lake.

Leaving the Alpine region behind via a short climb to Burke Pass, the road made a long descent towards the lowlands known as the Canterbury Plains. We turned off at Fairlie and cut across to join highway 1, the main road to Christchurch. The mountains had been replaced by patches of woods and the large cultivated fields of South Island's main agricultural region. Heading north on highway 1, we passed through Ashburton and numerous other farming communities. The place had a more English feel about it now. The mountains and wild forests were far away and the farms looked well kept and prosperous. We planned to stop just outside Christchurch rather than find a site in town and we finally pulled off the main highway at a camping sign just after an attractive looking pub set back from the road.

There seemed to be quite a few vans and caravans on here but many were in storage and unoccupied. The pub had proved attractive enough to walk back to, to have our evening meal there and we were glad we did. The place reminded me of a 'proper local' like the pub I'd sometimes go to with my Dad back home when I was visiting. This was where the local farmers came to chill out over a beer after a days work in the fields. An unpretentious bar with no loud music just a couple of fruit machines at one end by the door. A guy was playing one of the machines and looked to be having difficulties staying on his stool.

The food portions were certainly designed for someone who'd worked outdoors all day and we each managed a little over half of the huge piles of food on our plates. I went and got another beer. The guy in the corner seemed to have fed his last pennies into the machine as he was now attempting to walk through the exit door. He managed it on about the third attempt as I rejoined Jacqui with our drinks.

It felt strange to be coming to the end of our trip. Travelling from place to place had almost become a way of life for us over the last month or so. A few beers were a way of escaping the fact that neither of us really wanted to go back to England yet and the warm friendly atmosphere in here was prolonging our holiday as much as possible. Feeling decidedly less than sober, we walked back to the van by torchlight and watched the evening's entertainment of a late arrival assembling a trailer tent in the next bay. The trailer tent is a strange piece of equipment, a kind of a cross between a tent and a caravan. Over another bottle of wine we added this new fourth variable to the old argument between tent, caravan and campervan but thanks to the wine after our evening in the pub we didn't really come to any conclusion – not that I can remember anyway!

A headache is a headache whether self inflicted or not and whether genuine or as in my case, the result of an accident with a bottle of wine, its effect is to make all jobs seem twice as hard. This is even truer when it's something you never really wanted to do in the first place. Reluctantly we packed our things back into cases and readied the van for the road, the last few miles to Christchurch. We didn't see much of Christchurch as we headed straight to the Apollo depot near the airport. Our drop off point was near to the Antarctic Experience Centre and had I known this I would have made the effort to get here earlier so I could have a look around. We'd just assumed it would be a trip into town between dropping the van off and catching our flight to Auckland so we just hadn't bothered.

The handover went smoothly, a cursory look for any obvious collision damage and a look at the fuel gauge and the gas bottle, more to check it was still there, I'm sure in the UK they'd have weighed the thing just to extract more money from us. There was nothing to pay. The gas bottle must have been nearly empty as it had lasted a month but they didn't charge us for what we'd used. Good on you, Apollo!

Jacqui wasn't very happy at 'giving up our house' and neither was I we both felt somewhat homeless as we walked silently with our bags into the airport terminal. I was reminded of that last night of the holidays when me and Gill, my sister, would go to bed knowing it was school the next day or of waking up on Boxing Day knowing it was another year to Christmas. I suppose the good things can't always last forever and that all journeys must eventually come to an end. Well, until the next time anyway.

Epilogue
Return to Spring

The sun sparkled brightly on the blue waters of Auckland Harbour as a yacht, its white sail ruffled gently by the breeze, made its way slowly along the coast not far from the shore. A little further out a gull drifted lazily on the light wind while far across the water, backed by the broad bulk of Rangitoto Island at its far side, a motor launch made its way purposefully towards the city's port, way over to the left. The salty tang of the sea mingled with the scents of spring drifting over from the trees and gardens lining the road behind. Many of the people walking along this tree lined promenade wore only light summer clothes. A few were in shorts and they had hardly a coat between them.

It wasn't winter any more. We'd caught our flight OK the day before from Christchurch and the aircraft had brought us back to springtime. Nicola had met us at the airport and that night we'd all gone out along with a couple of her housemates to a Japanese restaurant in downtown Auckland. It had been a night of good food and good conversation coupled with plenty of Sake, which had lifted our end of holiday moods somewhat.

We were due to go to the airport again shortly to catch our flight back home so we'd come on a walk along the sea front to stock up on fresh air before nearly 2 days at sealed aircraft cabins and climate controlled departure lounges. Neither of us was looking forward to the whole thing. It wasn't that I don't like flying; I actually enjoy that part, though 12000 miles was pushing things a bit. It's all the getting there 2 hours before take off, the queuing up to check in and the waiting around I can't stand. Once I can hear the engines, I'm okay.

That morning's breakfast had been out of the ordinary to say the least. When I have pancakes at home I have them with lemon, sugar and bramble jam but when everyone at the house had elected to do pancakes for breakfast it was something completely different. We had them with bacon and yes, banana. Bacon and banana with maple syrup added to taste! Apparently this was the latest thing to have in Auckland. Either that or we were being wound up! Everyone seemed to enjoy it though so I suspect not. Actually, though unusual, the taste wasn't that bad, however next Shrove Tuesday I'll still be making sure that we have some lemons and bramble jam in the cupboard.

I think we'd managed most of what we'd planned for the trip and some more. OK we hadn't got to Stewart Island and the so called Great Walks or tramping tracks were a summer thing. I had however climbed Ruapehu which I'd thought also thought was a summer route and Jacqui had been skiing again. We'd seen Fiordland, the Southern Alps and the great cities of Auckland and Wellington. We'd met wildlife and encountered some great characters and I'd returned to Auckland a non-smoker. The things that we hadn't done were perhaps the best reason to come back.

The sound of a plane caught my attention. The aircraft was performing a banking turn far out over the harbour as it began a final approach to the airport. I looked at my watch – it was time to go.